Nutrition and Feeding of the Handicapped Child

To the memory of Janice

Nutrition and Feeding of the Handicapped Child

Edited by

Iris M. Crump, R.D., M.S.

San Diego Regional Center for the
Developmentally Disabled
San Diego, California

Illustrations by
Denise Dorricott

A College-Hill Publication
Little, Brown and Company
Boston/Toronto/San Diego

College-Hill Press
A division of
Little, Brown and Company (Inc.)
34 Beacon Street
Boston, Massachusetts 02108

Library of Congress Cataloging in Publication Data
Main entry under title:

Crump, Iris M.
  Nutrition and feeding of the handicapped child.
  Includes index.
  1. Handicapped children — Nutrition. 2. Handicapped
youth — Nutrition. 3. Handicapped children — Diseases —
Nutritional aspects. 4. Handicapped youth — Diseases —
Nutritional aspects. 5. School children — Food.
I. Title. [DNLM: 1. Child Nutrition. 2. Education,
Special. 3. Handicapped. 4. Mental Retardation.
5. Nutrition Disorders — in infancy & childhood.
WS 115 C956n]
RJ233.C78 1986   613.2′0880814   86-17641
ISBN 0-316-16384-8

ISBN 0-316-16384-8

Printed in the United States of America.

RJ233
·C78
1987
copy 1

Contents

List of Forms

Foreword

At long last a much needed resource book about nutrition and handi-capped children has been written. While this area has been addressed in occasional journal articles, papers, conferences, and symposia it has lacked the attention it deserves when one considers the pervasive effect nutrition can have on the life of any child. If we are indeed to educate and treat the "whole child" it is sensible that we understand all the parameters within which they exist. Nutrition as one of these parameters has been long overlooked or ignored in spite of its potential lifelong effects.

The author of this text, Iris Crump, has the sensitivity, impeccable credentials, and experience to move the reader from basic nutritional information to dissecting the varied facts and fallacies commonly associated with the interactions and influences of nutrition on functioning. From a description of the eating process, including anatomy, to an assessment of eating and guidelines of interventions, the reader is presented with a wealth of long-sought-after information that relates to the nutritional needs of the handicapped.

Very expertly and in an easily read style, Crump examines the effects of congenital disorders and those conditions which require special dietary management on nutrition. Adding to this wealth of information are the author's program suggestions for weight control, school mealtimes, and nutrition education programs applicable in the classroom and in a student's Individual Education Plan (IEP). Throughout the text the reader is free to use or adapt many of the recommended materials which have proven to be successful in other programs. The book concludes with a description of nutrition programs advocated or provided by private agencies and/or trade associations.

For readers who may ask, "Why do we need all this information on nutrition and the handicapped?" I would ask that they focus on the types of handicapped children now entering infant, preschool, and school programs. These children, like their nonhandicapped peers, are often under- or overfed, lacking in basic nutritional information, and unaware of the dangers involved in following a lifetime pattern of poor nutrition. In addition to those with a general disregard for good nutrition and health are those handicapped children who present gastrointestinal disorders (i.e., rumination, constipation, diarrhea), infectious diseases, malnutrition, and allergies.

It is my hope, and that of others in this complex field of educating the handicapped, that the special educator and regular class teacher, school nurse or health professional, dietitian, and all therapists and support staff who work with the handicapped, will review and become familiar with the materials, information, and suggested resources included in this book. The need for nutritional awareness, especially by those who work with handicapped children and their concomitant problems, will only escalate as these children move toward their rightful and full participation in society.

Michael Bender, Ed.D.
Director of Special Education
The Kennedy Institute
Associate Professor of Education and Pediatrics
Johns Hopkins University and School of Medicine

Preface

Teachers and other school staff have been trained to identify the learning needs and abilities of their students in order to provide them with an appropriate educational program. However, teachers in special education have an additional challenge, in that they must employ knowledge of how handicapping conditions are expressed in the learning process. As an example, one handicapping condition frequently found among students in special education is malnutrition. A relationship between nutrition and learning has been assumed throughout history. However, it was not documented clearly until Cravioto, in 1963, reported studies of the influence of protein–calorie malnutrition on psychological test behavior in Mexico.* In most children, developmental quotients increased with improved nutrition. A direct association was reported between deficits in height and weight of malnourished children, on the one hand, and retardation in language, adaptive, psychomotor, and personal and social behavior, on the other. Since that time, many aspects of nutritional influences on learning and behavior have been examined.

Malnutrition may be caused by a motor, mental, sensory, gastrointestinal, or metabolic disturbance. The disturbed function, in turn, may be caused by a congenital defect of the physical structure, such as cleft palate or micrognathia. Genetic disorders, illness, and drug treatment are among causes of altered nutrient requirements. Indulgence, ignorance, and lack of financial resources for appropriate intervention compound the existing complex problems.

The main purpose of *Nutrition and Feeding of the Handicapped Child* is to provide teachers, therapists, nurses, and other school staff members with information that will help them to improve the nutritional status of their handicapped students. For the purposes of this book, a child will be considered handicapped if she or he manifests any condition

---

* Cravioto, J. (1963). Application of newer knowledge of nutrition on physical and mental growth and development. *American Journal of Public Health, 53,* 1803.

that impairs a normal action or function. The handicapping condition may be mental or physical, and may include a combination of several disorders. Evaluation and individual program planning is necessary for each child.

This book examines what and how handicapped children eat. Methods for making mealtime a positive experience for both the child and the person responsible for feeding will be discussed. Experienced specialists have contributed their expertise in several chapters, to help readers achieve a greater understanding regarding nutritional problems of handicapped children, so they will be better equipped to help correct those problems.

My heartfelt thanks go to Michael Bender, Ed.D., who recognized the importance of emphasizing the nutrition needs of students in special education. He acknowledged my experience, encouraged my contribution, and guided my writing. The contributing authors have given generously of their expertise; this book would be incomplete without their input.

I want to thank Carolyn Porter for her competent typing and suggestions on format. A student at San Diego State University created the word search game included in Chapter 1, in partial completion of the course Diet Therapy, and another student supplied the illustrations.

This book is the outcome, also, of the collaboration of the staffs of many schools in San Diego and Imperial Counties, who demonstrated the effectiveness of nutrition intervention.

I have had the privilege of working with the excellent interdisciplinary staff of the San Diego Regional Center for the Developmentally Disabled for 15 years. Each of these colleagues has enriched my knowledge and effectiveness in providing services for our clients and educating the community concerning their nutritional needs and cares.

Iris M. Crump

Contributors

Kathryn Brune, B.S.
Family Health Project,
University of California, San Diego,
San Diego, California

James O. Cleveland, Ed.D.
Adjunct Professor, School of Education,
University of San Diego;
Director of Educational Services,
San Diego Regional Center for the Developmentally Disabled,
San Diego, California

Iris M. Crump, M.S., R.D.
Adjunct Professor,
Department of Family Studies and Consumer Sciences,
San Diego State University;
Nutrition Consultant,
San Diego Regional Center for the Developmentally Disabled,
San Diego, California

Barbara E. Gunning, Ph.D., R.D.
Professor, Foods and Nutrition,
Department of Family Studies and Consumer Sciences,
San Diego State University,
San Diego, California

Cornelia Lieb-Lundell, M.A., R.P.T.
Physical Therapy Consultant,
San Diego Regional Center for the Developmentally Disabled,
San Diego, California

Amy G. Salomon, M.A., C.C.C.-Sp.
Speech-Language-Hearing Consultant,
San Diego Regional Center for the Developmentally Disabled,
San Diego, California

CHAPTER 1

Nutrition of the Child and Adolescent

Barbara E. Gunning

Human mental and physical development are determined by inherited characteristics that are modified by the quality of nutrient intake. A positive effect on development is determined by both food selection and a modest supplement program when recommended by the attending pediatrician or health care provider. Negative developmental effects become apparent with the introduction of poor food choices, excess supplements, drugs, and such environmental factors as toxic waste and poor air control.

Nutrition is a composite of the knowledge that defines chemicals, hereafter referred to as nutrients, that are found in our food, and how these nutrients influence growth, development, and body maintenance.

The human body is capable of synthesizing many essential nutrients, while others must be taken orally. Essential nutrients that must be supplied by food are shown in Table 1–1.

Specific recommendations for nutrient intake levels in the United States are determined by the Food and Nutrition Board of the National Academy of Sciences. The most recent values are provided in Table 1–2. These are reviewed every 5 or 6 years, and summarize updated dietary studies. The Recommended Daily

1

Table 1–1. Essential Nutrients as Classified in 1985

Carbohydrate	*Protein (essential amino acids*)*
glucose	leucine
	isoleucine
Fat	lysine
linoleic	methionine
Minerals	phenylalanine
calcium	threonine
phosphorus	tryptophan
sulfur	valine
chlorine	histidine
magnesium	nonessential nitrogen
iron	
selenium	*Vitamins (fat soluble)*
zinc	A (retinol)
manganese	D (cholecalciferol)
copper	E (tocopherol)
cobalt	K
molydenum	*Vitamins (water soluble)*
iodine	thiamin
chromium	riboflavin
vanadium	niacin
tin	biotin
nickel	folacin
silicon	vitamin B_6
	vitamin B_{12}
	pantothenic acid
	vitamin C
	Water

*Protein building blocks

Dietary Allowances (RDA) have been determined as safe levels for most normal persons under usual environmental stresses in the United States of America.

Nutritional excesses offer no positive effect for the normal individual, and some nutrients, such as niacin, vitamins B_6, A (retinol), and D, may be detrimental or toxic if large excesses are consumed frequently.

Additional nutrients have been categorized as essential and must be included in the daily dietary intake. Precise requirements have not been established and will not be available until additional research is available for safety assurance. Table 1–3 provides a summary of estimated adequate and safe levels for these nutrients.

The incidence of pregnancy and lactation is quite high in the

Table 1-2. Recommended Dietary Allowances* Designed for the Maintenance of Good Nutrition

Age and Sex Group (yr)	Weight (kg)	(lb)	Height (cm)	(in.)	Protein (g)	Fat-Soluble Vitamins			Water-Soluble Vitamins							Minerals					
						Vitamin A (μg R.E.)†	Vitamin D (μg)‡	Vitamin E (mg α-T.E.)§	Vitamin C (mg)	Thiamin (mg)	Riboflavin (mg)	Niacin (mg-N.E.)	Vitamin B6 (mg)	Folacin (μg)††	Vitamin B12 (μg)‡‡	Calcium (mg)	Phosphorus (mg)	Magnesium (mg)	Iron (mg)	Zinc (mg)	Iodine (μg)
Children																					
1-3	13	29	90	35	23	400	10	5	45	0.7	0.8	9	0.9	100	2.0	800	800	150	15	10	70
4-6	20	44	112	44	30	500	10	6	45	0.9	1.0	11	1.3	200	2.5	800	800	200	10	10	90
7-10	28	62	132	52	34	700	10	7	45	1.2	1.4	16	1.6	300	3.0	800	800	250	10	10	120
Males																					
11-14	45	99	157	62	45	1,000	10	8	50	1.4	1.6	18	1.8	400	3.0	1,200	1,200	350	18	15	150
15-18	66	145	176	69	56	1,000	10	10	60	1.4	1.7	18	2.0	400	3.0	1,200	1,200	400	18	15	150
19-22	70	154	177	70	56	1,000	7.5	10	60	1.5	1.7	19	2.2	400	3.0	800	800	350	10	15	150
Females																					
11-14	46	101	157	62	46	800	10	8	50	1.1	1.3	15	1.8	400	3.0	1,200	1,200	300	18	15	150
15-18	55	120	163	64	46	800	10	8	60	1.1	1.3	14	2.0	400	3.0	1,200	1,200	300	18	15	150
19-22	55	120	163	64	44	800	7.5	8	60	1.1	1.3	14	2.0	400	3.0	800	800	300	18	15	150

*The allowances are intended to provide for individual variations among most normal persons as they live in the United States under usual environmental stresses. Diets should be based on a variety of common foods in order to provide other nutrients for which human requirements have been less well defined.

†Retinol equivalents; 1 retinol equivalent = 1 μg retinol or 6 μg B-carotene.

‡As cholecalciferol: 10 μg cholecalciferol = 400 I.U. vitamin D.

§α tocopherol equivalents: 1 mg D-α-tocopherol = 1 α T.E.

**N.E. (niacin equivalent) = 1 mg niacin to 60 mg dietary tryptophan.

††The folacin allowances refer to dietary sources as determined by Lactobacillus casei assay after treatment with enzymes ("conjugases") to make polyglutamyl forms of the vitamin available to the test organism.

‡‡The RDA for vitamin B_{12} in infants is based on average concentration of the vitamin in human milk. The allowances after weaning are based on energy intake (as recommended by the American Academy of Pediatrics) and consideration of other factors, such as intestinal absorption.

From the Food and Nutrition Board, National Academy of Sciences, National Research Council, revised 1980.

3

Table 1-3. Estimated Safe and Adequate Daily Dietary Intakes of Additional Selected Vitamins and Minerals*†

	Age (years)	Vitamin K (µg)	Biotin (µg)	Pantothe- nic Acid (mg)	Copper (mg)	Mangan- ese (mg)
Infants	0 – 0.5	12	35	2	0.5 – 0.7	0.5 – 0.7
	0.5 – 1	10 – 20	50	3	0.7 – 1.0	0.7 – 1.0
Children and	1 – 3	15 – 30	65	3	1.0 – 1.5	1.0 – 1.5
Adolescents	4 – 6	20 – 40	85	3 – 4	1.5 – 2.0	1.5 – 2.0
	7 – 10	30 – 60	120	4 – 5	2.0 – 2.5	2.0 – 3.0
	11 +	50 – 100	100 – 200	4 – 7	2.0 – 3.0	2.5 – 5.0
Adults		70 – 140	100 – 200	4 – 7	2.0 – 3.0	2.5 – 5.0

*Because there is less information on which to base allowances, these figures are not given in the main table of the RDA and are provided here in the form of ranges of recommmended intakes.

†Since the toxic levels for many trace elements may be only several times usual intakes, the upper levels for the trace elements given in this table should not be habitually exceeded.

teenage population of the United States. In these conditions, additional nutrients are essential, and an appropriately amended table should be consulted.

DETERMINATION OF ENERGY NEEDS

The discussion of energy is based on kilocalorie needs or available energy stored in food eaten and released for the body's use after the bound food chemicals are metabolized and utilized. Energy must be available for growth, development, and activity. These needs vary with age, sex, culture, heredity, environmental temperature, activity, and other factors. Each individual must be considered independently of other persons when predicting kilocalorie needs. Therefore, it should be expected that a wide range of values will represent the varied needs of an entire population, as is shown in Table 1–4.

During growth, energy needs are very high, but wise food choices should be of paramount concern when selecting foods to satisfy these energy needs. Children should be discouraged from consuming foods with "empty calories," a term that describes foods containing nothing but calories, exclusive of other nutrients, of which sugar is a typical example.

Excess calories lead to overweight, which is a disorder among all classes of people. Overweight persons are not necessarily better nourished than thin persons, because their food choices may not provide all essential nutrients. Overweight conditions must be

Fluoride (mg)	Chromium (mg)	Selenium (mg)	Molybdenum (mg)	Sodium (mg)	Potassium (mg)	Chloride (mg)
0.1 – 0.5	0.01 – 0.04	0.01 – 0.04	0.03 – 0.06	115 – 350	350 – 925	275 – 700
0.2 – 1.0	0.02 – 0.06	0.02 – 0.06	0.04 – 0.08	250 – 750	425 – 1275	400 – 1200
0.5 – 1.5	0.02 – 0.08	0.02 – 0.08	0.05 – 0.1	325 – 975	550 – 1650	500 – 1500
1.0 – 2.5	0.03 – 0.12	0.03 – 0.12	0.06 – 0.15	450 – 1350	775 – 2325	700 – 2100
1.5 – 2.5	0.05 – 0.2	0.05 – 0.2	0.1 – 0.3	600 – 1800	1000 – 3000	925 – 2775
1.5 – 2.5	0.05 – 0.2	0.05 – 0.2	0.15 – 0.5	900 – 2700	1525 – 4575	1400 – 4200
1.5 – 4.0	0.05 – 0.2	0.05 – 0.2	0.15 – 0.5	1100 – 3300	1875 – 5625	1700 – 5100

Reproduced from: Recommended Dietary Allowances, Ninth Edition, 1980, with permission of the National Academy of Sciences, Washington, D.C.

discouraged; a fat child is not a healthy child. Children should eat a variety of foods of high nutrient density, meaning optimal nutrients per calorie of food.

NUTRITIONAL DEFICIENCIES

How is a nutritional deficiency shown? The answer is frequently subjective, and thus dependent upon a care-giver's alertness and constant surveillance of the children in their care. Nutritional deficiencies generally do not evidence themselves objectively until they are quite advanced. Thus, a two-pronged set of guidelines can be established to relate to both subjective and objective observations:

Subjective observation should alert the care-giver that a nutritional problem is evident and must be evaluated. It can then, hopefully, be corrected before it becomes an overt illness requiring extensive evaluation and remediation. Table 1–5 provides clues to the nutritional status of the child being observed. No one characteristic should be used as definitive; prior to assuming that the diet is either adequate or inadequate, a number of characteristics must be observed and evaluated.

Objective observations are more definitive, but also difficult to interpret unless a specific deficiency is present. Specific nutrient deficiencies are unusual because foods contain many nutrients that interact with each other and are rarely isolated as uniquely responsible for clinical deficiency states. Nevertheless, efforts have been successful in distinguishing the subjective characteristics of many nutritional deficiencies, as well as the effects of excesses.

Table 1–4. National Research Council, Recommended Daily Dietary Allowances, Mean Heights and Weights and Recommended Energy Intake*

Category	Age (yr)	Weight (kg)	Weight (lb)	Height (cm)	Height (in.)	Energy needs (range) (kcal)	
Children	1–3	13	29	90	35	1300	(900–1800) 5.5
	4–6	20	44	112	44	1700	(1300–2300) 7.1
	7–10	28	62	132	52	2400	(1650–3300) 10.1
Males	11–14	45	99	157	62	2700	(2000–3700) 11.3
	15–18	66	145	176	69	2800	(2100–3900) 11.8
	19–22	70	154	177	70	2900	(2500–3300) 12.2
Females	11–14	46	101	157	62	2200	(1500–3000) 9.2
	15–18	55	120	163	64	2100	(1200–3000) 8.8
	19–22	55	120	163	64	2100	(1700–2500) 8.8

*Adapted from *Recommended dietary allowances*, Ninth Edition (1980). Food and Nutrition Board, National Academy of Science, Washington, D.C.

Energy allowances for children through age 18 are based on median energy intakes of children of these ages followed in longitudinal growth studies. Values in parentheses are 10th and 90th percentiles of energy intake, to indicate the range of energy consumption among children of these ages.

Table 1–5. Clinical Signs of Nutritional Status of Children

Signs	Well nourished	Poorly nourished
Attitude	Alert, good endurance	Listless, irritable, poor attention span, tires easily
Hair	Lustrous, with clean scalp	Dull, brittle, thin, scaly, sore scalp
Skin	Clear, even color, smooth	Scaly, greasy with sores, bruises, petechia
Lips	Pink, moist	Pale, swollen, with lesions
Teeth	Even, clean white	Carious, mottled, with plaque buildup
Tongue	Pink color, surface papillae, no lesions	Atrophy of papillae, smooth or swollen or red
Gums	Pink, moist, firm	Spongy, pale or red, with sores or bleeding
Posture	Erect, firm musculature	Humped, with protruding abdomen
Bone structure	No malformations	Large joints, bow legs, beaded ribs, abnormal chest
Body build	Appropriate weight for height	Over- or underweight
Gastrointestinal function	Good appetite and digestion, normal, regular bowel function	Anorexia, abnormal hunger or thirst, gas expulsion, vomiting, diarrhea, or constipation

FUNCTION AND FOOD SOURCES OF NUTRIENTS

In order to effectively use our nutrition knowledge, it is necessary to translate this information into nutrient composition of food. Food selection is a key phrase that can be utilized to provide the person with a well-balanced diet of adequate calories and nutrients that will support optimal growth and development and still have plenty to spare for desired activity.

Foods can be divided into five groups and key nutrients found in each group are summarized in Table 1–6. Some essential nutrients listed in Table 1–1 do not appear here because they are found in many foods or are needed in such small quantities that it is literally impossible to eliminate them from a normal diet. Table 1–7 contains a more comprehensive summary of nutrients

Table 1–6. Key Nutrients From Food Groups

Food Group	Key Nutrients
Milk and milk products	Calcium, phosphorus, riboflavin (vitamin B_2), cobalamin (vitamin B_{12}), protein
Meat, fish, poultry, eggs, legumes, nuts	Zinc, phosphorus, iron, pyridoxine (vitamin B_6), vitamin B_{12}, protein
Fruits and vegetables	Retinol (vitamin A), ascorbic acid (vitamin C), vitamin B_6
Breads and cereals (whole or enriched grains and flour)	Complex carbohydrates, vitamin-B complex including thiamin (vitamin B_1), riboflavin (vitamin B_2), niacin (vitamin B_3), minerals including iron, calcium, magnesium, zinc
Other foods that contribute calories only	Fats and simple carbohydrates (sugars)

and their major functions. This table provides the more specific foods than include major nutrients needed by all persons. Other nutrients listed on Tables 1–1 and 1–3 generally accompany the items listed on Table 1–7 of foods that provide quantities appropriate for performance of their known physiological function. If basic nutrients are not supplied by food, but rather by a concentrated supplement, the minute but essential minerals and trace elements are inadequate. Using the best food sources, therefore, provides high nutrient density for a well-balanced diet.

The final concern we all have relates to what food patterns will assure normal growth and development. Table 1–8 lists suggested daily intake for independent family planning based on preferences, availability, and cost. Table 1–9 provides recommendations about number and size of food servings for various age groups.

For those in mid- to late adolescence, additional considerations must be evaluated that make it meaningless to include in Table 1–8. Growth may be decreasing, and changes in body development need to be considered on an individual basis to determine daily nutrient and energy needs. This is a period in which it is difficult to categorically make recommendations. Also, adolescents exhibit independence in food choices. They select foods that taste good to them, and are frequently on weight-control diets to lose weight, remain thin, or modify body mass for selected sports.

Lean body mass is similar in the prepuberty male and female, but changes rapidly with the final growth spurt of adolescence.

At that time, the female develops a higher percentage of body fat, and the male has an increase in lean body mass. Lean body mass is related to an increase in blood volume that requires increased iron intake; the female also needs additional iron as a result of menses.

Many persons in this age group avoid breakfast, which may have a net effect of decreasing caloric intake and blood glucose. Fatigue, decreased mental acuity, and irritability can be evidenced.

Each young person is dependent upon individual genetic predisposition for typical growth and development. In addition, many environmental factors must be considered. Persons who consume either legal or illegal drugs will frequently experience nutritional stress. Aspirin alters vitamin C activity, and quantities somewhat greater than those in the RDA are needed if aspirin is taken daily. Children who spend their growing years in a cold climate will not have the full advantage of the sunshine vitamin D and will require more of this nutrient in their diet than the child who is exposed to large amounts of indirect sunlight. Also, alcohol ingestion decreases the intestinal absorption of several nutrients such as thiamin and folic acid. Consequently, more of the foods containing these nutrients are needed if alcohol is ingested regularly.

Teenage pregnancy places stress on the developing fetus, as well as growth of the pregnant girl. This, combined with a desire to be "thin," may lead to inadequate nutritional availability and deficiencies.

The individual must be the major focus when determining eating patterns that will provide adequate nutrition. Good nutrition is a result of chemical constituents consumed orally, optimal absorption, and ultimate utilization of these chemicals that we classify as nutrients.

These factors do not suggest the use of large increases in nutrients, as excesses are as detrimental as slight deficiencies in many cases. The RDAs presented in Table 1–2 are those for the United States and are higher than the recommended dietary intakes of many countries. The RDAs have a built-in safety factor that provides for genetic, environmental, and physiological variations.

The saying "A happy child is a healthy child" is useful in judging nutritional status, because good nutrition promotes a feeling of vibrant wellness that contributes to the young person's optimal performance and enjoyment of life. Ways to teach the young student to make wise food choices can be inserted into many areas of their study. In Chapter 9, "Curriculum for the Classroom," approaches are offered. Also, Appendix 1–1 is a game that can encourage consumption of healthful foods. Many posters,

Table 1–7. Nutrient Functions and Best Food Sources

Nutrient	Major Functions	Best Food Sources
	Fuel Nutrients	
Protein (provides essential amino acids)	Tissue growth Tissue repair Antibody formation Body regulator Hormone synthesis Energy production	Eggs; milk and cheese; fish; poultry; meat; soybeans; dry beans; nuts
Carbohydrate simple, complex	Energy production	Fruits; vegetables; breads and cereals; sugar products; milk (lactose)
Fat	Energy production Soluble vitamin transport Thermal insulation Internal organ cushion	Cooking oil; salad dressing; butter or margarine; nuts
	Nutrient Transport	
Fiber	Good bowel elimination	Fruits; vegetables; whole grains
Water	Cell structure maintenance Water soluble nutrient transport Waste products carrier	Fluids; foods
	Water Soluble Vitamins	
Thiamin (B$_1$)	Energy release Nervous system maintenance	Pork and lean meat; beans; seeds; peas; whole grain and enriched breads and cereals
Riboflavin (B$_2$)	Energy release	Milk and yogurt; cheese; whole grains and enriched breads and cereals; organ means
Niacin (B$_3$)	Energy release Maintenance of healthy skin	Meat; chicken; milk; egg; banana
Pyridoxine (B$_6$)	Maintenance of neurological systems Prevention of anemia	Organ meats; banana; avocado; meat – poultry; fish

(continued)

Table 1—7 *(continued)*

Folic acid (Folacin)	Prevention of anemia	Liver; green vegetables; oranges
Cobalamin (B_{12})	Prevention of anemia Nervous system function	Beef; liver; seafood; eggs; milk; primarily animal sources
Ascorbic acid (C)	Collagen formation Infection fighting Wound healing	Citrus fruit; broccoli; strawberry; cantaloupe; baked potato

Fat Soluble Vitamins

Retinol (A) Carotenes (A)	Maintenance of soft smooth skin Maintenance of mucous membranes to provide resistance to infection Protection against night blindness by promoting healthy eyes	Liver; dark green or orange vegetables; yellow/orange fruit; butter; fortified margerine whole milk; fortified nonfat milk; eggs
Vitamin D ("Sunshine" vitamin)	Calcium absorption Bone and other hard tissue growth and maintenance	Salmon; milk, whole and D-fortified; tuna; liver

Select Minerals

Calcium	Bone growth and maintenance Teeth growth and maintenance Promotion of blood clotting Maintenance of normal muscle action	Milk; cheese; canned salmon; sesame seeds cheddar cheese
Iron	Maintenance of red blood cells for transport of oxygen	Liver; meat; prunes; raisins; whole grains; molasses; egg
Iodine	Thyroxin production	Iodized salt; seafood

Several very important nutrients have not been included in summary. These nutrients include the water-soluble vitamins, pantothenic acid, and biotin, plus the fat-soluble vitamin K. The term pantothenate has been cited as the nutrient that is "everywhere." It would thus be a rare situation to have a specific deficiency. Biotin and vitamin K are primarily synthesized by intestinal bacteria and a deficiency of either nutrient is so rare that it would be considered a nutritional abnormality that needs to be evaluated by the dietitian and physician.

Table 1–8. Recommended Food Intake for Good Nutrition According to Food Groups and the Average Size of Servings at Different Age Levels

Food Group	Servings/Day	Average Size of Servings					
		1 yr	2–3 yr	4–5 yr	6–9 yr	10–12 yr	13–15 yr
Milk and cheese (1.5 oz cheese = 1 c milk (C = 1 cup – 8 oz or 240 g))	4	½ c	½–¾ c	¾ c	¾ c	1 c	1 c
Meat group (protein foods)	3						
Eggs		1	1	1	1	1	1
Lean meat, fish, poultry (liver once a week)		2 tbsp	2 tbsp	4 tbsp	2–3 oz (4–6 tbsp)	3–4 oz	4 oz or more
Peanut butter			1 tbsp	2 tbsp	2–3 tbsp	3 tbsp	3 tbsp
Fruits and vegetables Vitamin C source (citrus fruits, berries, tomato, cabbage, cantaloupe)	At least 4, including: 1 or more (twice as much tomato as citrus)	⅓ c citrus	½ c	½ c	1	1	1

Food	Servings						
Vitamin A source (green or yellow fruits and vegetables)	1	2 tbsp	3 tbsp	4 tbsp (¼ c)	¼ c	⅓ c	½ c
Other vegetables (potatoes and legumes) or	2	2 tbsp	3 tbsp	4 tbsp (¼ c)	⅓ c	½ c	¾ c
Other fruits (apple, banana, etc.)		¼ c	⅓ c	½ c	1 medium	1 medium	1 medium
Cereals (whole-grain or enriched)	At least 4						
Breads; tortillas; crackers;		½ c	1 slice	1½ slice	1–2 slices	2 slices	2 slices
Ready-to-eat cereals;		½ oz	¾ oz	1 oz	1 oz	1 oz	1 oz
Cooked cereal (including macaroni, spaghetti, rice, etc.)		¼ c	⅓ c	½ c	½ c	¾ c	1 c or more
Fats and carbohydrates	To meet caloric needs						
Butter, margarine, mayonaise, oils, sugars							

Adapted from Four Food Groups of the Daily Food Guide, Institute of Home Econmics, U.S. Department of Agriculture; and Publication #30, Children's Bureau of the United States Department of Health, Education, and Welfare.

Table 1–9. Recommended Number and Size of Food Servings by Age Level

Serving Size	Food Groups	Number of Servings			
		2–4 yr	5–8 yr	9–12 yr	13–15 yr
8 oz 2 C	*Milk group* Milk or yogurt; 1 ½ oz cheese Cottage cheese, 1 ⅓ C ice cream	3	4	5	4–5
2 oz 1 C	*Meat group* Meat, poultry or fish; 2 eggs Beans or 4 tbsp peanut butter	1	2	2	3–4
1 piece 1 C ½ C	*Cereal group* Breads, tortilla, pita, bagel Ready-to-eat cereal, popcorn Cooked cereal, rice, pasta, grits	2	3	4	4–7
1 ea ½ C	*Fruit & vegetable group:* include Green pepper, orange, grapefruit, broccoli, brussel sprouts, strawberries, papaya	½	1	1	2
½ C	Sweet potato, carrots, spinach, watermelon, cantaloupe, apricots	½	½	1	1
1 ea	Corn, potato, summer squash	1	2	2	2
as needed	*Other group* (principally calories) Fats: vegetable oil, butter margarine, salad dressings, sour or whipped cream Sweets: candy, desserts, sweetened beverages	To meet energy needs			

From "Four Groups of the Daily Food Guide," Institute of Home Economics, United States Department of Agriculture.

games, and curriculum materials are available from the organizations listed in Chapter 9. Projects and papers to send home can support the student's new food preferences and benefit the whole family as well.

BIBLIOGRAPHY

American Diabetes Association, Inc. (1976). *The ADA: Exchange lists for meal planning.* Chicago: The American Dietetic Association.

Guthrie, H. A. (1980). *Introductory nutrition from childhood through adulthood.* St. Louis: Times Mirror/Mosby, p. 559.

Recommended dietary allowance, Ninth Edition (1980). Washington DC: National Academy of Sciences.

Human nutrition information service administrative report (1985). Hyattsville, MD: United States Department of Agriculture, p. 377.

HEALTHY AFTERSCHOOL
SNACKS — WORD SEARCH

How many healthy and unhealthy afterschool snacks can you find in the word search diagram? When you find the word in the diagram, circle it, then cross it off the list. All words are found in a straight line either forward, backward, up, down or diagonally. No letter is ever skipped. You will not use up every letter in the diagram.

G	F	H	B	N	F	C	D	S	K	C	I	T	S	T	O	R	R	A	C
O	Y	E	V	L	M	R	P	M	T	Y	U	Y	E	F	A	D	N	V	X
C	S	K	C	I	T	S	Y	R	E	L	E	C	K	I	V	R	V	D	M
N	L	O	B	Z	O	R	W	P	K	U	Z	G	S	X	Z	P	P	F	O
C	E	V	X	C	A	N	D	Y	B	A	R	I	A	S	Z	U	O	H	Q
B	Z	T	G	E	P	O	P	C	O	R	N	J	S	E	Y	L	P	S	S
D	T	N	L	F	P	F	E	D	T	S	R	A	R	K	G	Y	S	K	U
O	E	H	R	M	L	N	A	G	P	B	N	K	B	A	R	Y	I	S	B
W	R	U	Y	K	E	G	N	U	E	A	T	S	Y	C	A	Z	C	T	D
H	P	A	I	T	S	H	U	K	N	Z	W	T	U	P	N	W	L	U	F
R	O	P	N	B	C	V	T	A	C	Z	B	N	S	U	O	T	E	N	G
T	A	U	H	G	H	U	B	N	U	E	W	K	T	C	L	R	S	O	I
E	V	T	D	V	E	Q	U	M	H	E	X	Z	D	X	A	S	X	D	K
A	E	K	A	C	B	S	T	R	U	G	O	Y	N	Z	N	D	Y	X	M
S	Z	D	O	H	Y	D	T	X	K	K	Y	X	O	C	H	I	P	S	O
M	R	L	Z	Q	C	H	E	E	S	E	W	E	D	G	E	S	C	P	Q
P	A	W	X	R	M	A	R	B	G	E	L	N	E	K	C	I	H	C	R

These will help you grow healthy and strong.

POPCORN
APPLES
PEANUT BUTTER
CARROT STICKS
BANANAS
RAISINS
CHEESE WEDGES
YOGURT
CELERY STICKS
ORANGES
GRANOLA
CHICKEN LEGS

Eating these too often is harmful to the body.

CHIPS
CANDY BARS
COLA
POPSICLES
CUPCAKES
CAKES
PRETZELS
DONUTS

CHAPTER 2

Interactions and Influences on Nutrient Function

Iris M. Crump

The educational environment is unique for observation of changes in the health, intellectual function, and behavior of students. Factors influencing those changes may involve nutrient intakes and their function. For example, the skilled teacher who is aware of behavior changes may intercept such problems as the student who has no breakfast and is, consequently, irritable and inattentive. Cleveland and Berkowitz (1975) emphasize, "if the child senses an empathetic understanding on behalf of the teacher, a good rapport and meaningful communication will be established."

In this chapter there will be a continuation of the discussion on the function of nutrients and their interaction with both drugs and other nutrients.

DRUG-NUTRIENT INTERACTION

The broad definition of a drug is that of any biologically active substance, natural or synthetic. Hormones, electrolytes, and vitamins enter this classification. In medical parlance, drugs are defined as therapeutic agents used in prevention, diagnosis, treatment, or cure of disease. Some nutrients are included in this category, such as the use of thiamin for megaloblastic anemia, or vitamin B12 used in cobalamin-dependent methylmalonic aciduria. These and other matabolic disorders are diagnosed and treated by physicians who specialize in management of inborn errors of metabolism.

While the pharmacist and health care provider must describe side-effects that may occur with the use of each drug they dispense, nutritional implications may be overlooked. The school nurse, teachers, and parents need to be aware of how to avoid deleterious effects of drug-nutrient interactions. Most drugs and nutrients are absorbed in the small intestine. Their interaction with all of the functions of the gastrointestinal tract are complicated and depend on drug dosage, type, and amount of food, as well as when each is taken. Disease and malnutrition are also damaging and are described in more detail in Chapter 6.

The six ways in which drugs interact with or influence the functions of nutrients are:

1. Increasing or decreasing food intake.
2. Inhibiting nutrient synthesis.
3. Decreasing absorption of nutrients.
4. Altering transport of metabolites.
5. Interfering with utilization or storage of metabolites
6. Increasing excretion of nutrients

These complex processes are not fully understood and studies of outcomes continue.

School staff will sometimes be perplexed by and concerned about a child's distorted perception of food. The child may reject or ignore food. The rejection may be due to reduced acuity of taste sensation, which is called hypogeusia, and such an alteration may be caused by any of the following drugs (Carson and Gormican, 1976):

Methylthiouracil	Meprobamate
Bentyl®	Phenytoin
Clofibrate	Penicillamine
Griseofulvin	Acetyl sulfosalyicylic acid

Additional taste distortions caused by drugs are a decrease in bitter and sweet sensitivity as a result of anesthesia, and an increase in bitter sensitivity on the part of the person taking amphetamines.

Other strong deterrents to eating are nausea and a dry mouth. The nonverbal child may not be able to express these kinds of discomforts. The school staff and family should be informed of these types of side-effects of drugs prescribed for the students; the school nurse could add suggestions to the student's daily program and discuss changes in eating behavior with the parents.

Observing the child's response during a food taste trial can help to distinguish individual reponses. The trial should be in a place and at a time other than mealtime to avoid the possible carry-over of the child's rejection of one taste to his or her rejection of an entire meal.

Volumes have been written on the effects of drugs on the body's secretory, digestive, absorptive, and metabolic systems. To collect information useful for care of students in special education, school nurses were surveyed by the authors to report the drugs prescribed most frequently for students in special classes. Following is a summary of some of the effects of those drugs on nutritional status. Therapeutic measures for treatment of deficiencies are not stated, but dietary measures needed to avoid nutritional deficits are shown in Table 2–1. The bibliography that follows this chapter gives what is known of the physiological mechanism and sequelae.

APPROPRIATE USE OF NUTRIENT SUPPLEMENTS

In some cases of drug-nutrient interaction, nutrient supplements are recommended (Table 2–1). The supplements recommended should ensure that recommended daily dietary allowances are fully provided. Need for additional supplementation should be discussed with a dietitian, pediatrician, or pharmacist. Other conditions in which supplements are recommended are discussed in Chapters 5 and 6. Additional factors that indicate a need for supplementation of the food intake are considered in this section.

Effects of Stress on Nutritional Needs

Many animal and human studies of stress response have been done. Stress is defined in Stedman's Medical Dictionary (1976, p. 1346) as "the reactions of the animal body to forces of a deleterious nature, infections and various abnormal states that tend to disturb its normal physiological equilibrium (homeostasis)."

Those stresses frequently experienced by persons with physical handicaps are respiratory and gastrointestinal infections, surgical procedures, cardiac incompetence, and the exertion in move-

Table 2–1. Drug and Nutrient Interactions

Major Drugs by Therapeutic Class	Possible Nutritional Effect	Prevention of Nutritional Effect	Possible Physical Effect
Analgesics			
Aspirin	Depresses serum vitamin C and folic acid. Increases urinary loss of vitamin C, potassium, and amino acids.	Add 50–100 mg/day vitamin C as in broccoli, citrus juice, strawberries. Increase fresh greens and raw fruits.	GI irritations; nausea dyspepsia; heartburn; prolonged bleeding time.
Antacids			
Maalox®	Decreases iron absorption, depresses serum phosphate.	Increase intake of liver, molasses, wheat germ, whole grains, peanuts, green vegetables.	Decreased stomach acidity; edema from high sodium content; constipation; steatorrhea.
Antibiotics			
Neomycin®	Decreases lactase activity.	Decrease milk intake or give "Lact-Aid."	Decreased appetite and taste acuity; diarrhea; nausea;
Chloramphenicol®	Hinders *all* intestinal absorption.	Give a well-balanced vitamin and mineral supplement and high-calorie fruit juice.	vomiting; general malabsorption of nutrients.
Tetracycline®		Decrease dairy products and give a calcium supplement.	
Anticonvulsants			
Phenobarbital Dilantin®	Disturbs vitamin D metabolism resulting in poor calcium utilization, producing osteoporosis and rickets.	Oral: 800 I.U. vitamin D daily, or calcitriol prescribed by an M.D.	Swelling of gums; G.I. distress; constipation; anorexia; osteomalacia.

(continued)

Table 2–1   *(continued)*

Major Drugs by Therapeutic Class	Possible Nutritional Effect	Prevention of Nutritional Effect	Possible Physical Effect
	Increases need for folic acid to prevent megaloblastic anemia. May lower blood level of vitamins K, B_6, and B_{12}.	Give 1–5 mg/day folic acid as in a multivitamin *tablet* (folic acid is *not* contained in liquid supplements). Daily vitamin B_{12}: RDA = 2 mg. Vitamin B_6: 10 mg/day for maintenance on drugs.	Contributes to megaloblastic anemia.
Antihypertensive			
Metala-zone®	Depresses serum potassium levels.	Feed foods high in potassium such as potatoes, bananas, carrots, celery, broccoli, and citrus fruits.	Thirst; anorexia; increased urine output; sugar/blood in urine; drowsiness; GI distress
Antitubercular			
Isoniazid®	Increases need for pyridoxine (vitamin B_6) and niacin (vitamin B_3)	Give a supplement of vitamin B complex. Increase foods such as meat, fish, poultry, eggs, and walnuts.	Possible hepatitis; hyperglycemia; anorexia; GI distress
Cathartics			
Mineral oil	Vitamins A, D, E, K absorbed in oil and excreted.	Give supplement of fat-soluble vitamins 12 hours after each dose of oil.	Abdominal cramps; steatorrhea; GI distress
Exlax®	Decreased absorption of vitamin D. Depletion of potassium. Poor nutrient absorption due to increased transit time.	Give multivitamin supplement if used regularly. Give liberal fruits and vegetables.	Abdominal cramps due to hyperperistalsis

(continued)

Table 2–1 *(continued)*

Major Drugs by Therapeutic Class	Possible Nutritional Effect	Prevention of Nutritional Effect	Possible Physical Effect
Corticosteroids			
Prednisone	Increases need for protein and vitamin B_6, C, D, and folic acid. Increases retention of sodium. Increases loss of potassium, calcium, and zinc	Give diet liberal in dairy products and meat. Restrict intake of salt (sodium). Give multiple vitamin-mineral supplement.	Edema and increased weight; weakness; dizziness; growth suppression in children; impaired wound healing; osteoporosis; GI distress; insulin-resistant; glucose intolerant
Diuretics			
Thiazides: (Diamox® Reserpine®)	Increases loss of potassium	See antihypertensive drugs	See antihypertensive drugs
Stimulants (CNS)			
Methylphenedate (Ritalin®) Dextroamphetamine (Dexedrine®)	Suppresses appetite and therefore growth.	Give drug *with* rather than *before* meals.* Reduce dosage to minimum required.	Decreased appetite, growth rate, and weight in children; nausea; dizziness; drowsiness
Sulfonamides			
	Promotes crystalization in bladder of large doses of vitamin C. Inhibits protein synthesis. Decreases serum folate and iron.	Avoid large supplements of vitamin C. Increase intake of eggs, meat, nuts, beans.	GI distress, dizziness; anorexia
Tranquilizers			
Mellaril®	Increases appetite to produce weight gain.	Monitor calories.	Increased weight; increased appetite; edema; dry mouth; drowsiness; constipation; GI distress; blurred vision

*See Table 6–3, p. 81, "More per Bite."

ment of spastic muscles. Stress places added demands on vitamin C and B-complex vitamins, all of which are water soluble and not stored in body tissues, as are the fat soluble vitamins. According to Goodhart and Shils (1973), human deficiencies of these vitamins are known to produce rapid fatigue, irritability, and loss of appetite (anorexia). Children in special education may have many of the stresses described, such as spastic musculature, increased exposure to infections, and decreased gastrointestinal and immunological integrity. For the child whose health is compromised, these factors suggest supplementation of the diet. A multivitamin containing both vitamin B complex and vitamin C containing 100 percent RDA could be given. Students who have no extraordinary stress and eat a varied diet that provides the RDA of nutrients do not need a vitamin supplement.

Megavitamin Concepts

It cannot be overemphasized that excesses of nutrient supplements do not improve functioning beyond that achieved by intakes that meet physiological needs. Many extensive studies were conducted from 1948 to 1958 concerning depletion and supplementation of nutrients (Foltz, Barboska, & Ivy, 1944; Grande, Anderson, & Kays, 1958). They report marked improvement when deficiencies were corrected but no change with additional supplementation. Excesses are excreted as rapidly as the kidney can filter them out of the body, with diarrhea assisting in getting rid of the offending substances. Homeostasis, the body's hard-working system of equilibrium control, is disturbed and may be damaged. For example, an adult intake of ascorbic acid (vitamin C) over the 500 milligrams that can be excreted daily can be harmful (Rhead and Schrauzer, 1971). It raises the urine uric acid level and may precipitate gout in persons predisposed to the disorder. Another undesirable effect of excessive vitamin C intake is rebound scurvy; because the body cannot use the excess ascorbic acid, it increases breakdown of the vitamin. This catabolic process continues even if the vitamin supplement is discontinued, so that symptoms of deficiency occur because the body's state of homeostasis has been disturbed. A gradual decrease of the megadose rather than abrupt discontinuation is therefore needed to re-establish normal function.

The reducing activity of excessive vitamin C can destroy vitamin B_{12} and cause false results for both urine sugar and blood-in-stool tests. Contraindications of excessive intake should be respected, especially since there is no significant clinically demonstrated benefit of megadoses of vitamin C to support its use.

Vitamin Function

A description of vitamin function may help to clarify its appropriate use as a supplement. Most vitamins acquired from food or supplements are transported to the cell sites where they convert to coenzymes, which attach to a protein called an apoenzyme. The product of each combination is a holoenzyme that catalyzes specific metabolic reactions. In this reaction, the enzyme accelerates the chemical reaction. The RDA in the United States approximate saturation of the apoenzymes. Body cells are limited in their production of apoenzyme, which also limits the amount of vitamin coenzyme that can bind with it to serve the vitamin function. As reported to the Committee on Nutritional Misinformation (1975), all excess vitamin then acts as a chemical that must be excreted, or, with fat-soluble vitamins A and D, is stored to potentially toxic levels.

Nutrients are vulnerable to misuse as panaceas (cure-alls) for all ailments because the recoveries from deficiency states are dramatic, and nutrient supplements are not controlled by law. For a condition in which a deficiency state is suspected, loading or balance studies can ascertain the body's status and predict appropriate prescription of supplements, if needed.

NUTRITIONAL ASPECTS OF HEALTH FOODS

Concern over harmful practices in agriculture and food processing are legitimate; steroids in animals and pesticides in plant crops have prompted public outcry that has been influential in providing laws and monitoring mechanisms to outlaw these practices, and has also spurred the development of "natural" foods. These products are altered as little as possible from the original plant or animal in its natural environment, with no synthetic ingredients or additives.

The principle is good, although occasionally dishonest, and costly marketing sometimes defiles the objective. There is no evidence of the nutritional superiority of organically grown crops; if the soil is deficient in nutrients, crop yield rather than the nutrient value of the plant will be the primary difference. Proper balance of soil nutrients may be provided by humus or compost, or these "natural" fertilizers may contain inadequate minerals or toxic contaminants.

VEGETARIAN DIETS

The popularity of vegetarian diets relates to ecological and ethical concerns, as well as the high cost of animal foods. There are several classifications of diets: the lacto-ovovegetarian diet consists of dairy products and eggs; the lactovegetarian diet uses plant foods and dairy products; and the pure vegetarian diet uses plant foods only. All of these diet regimens can be nutritionally adequate, although the pure vegetarian must be knowledgeable about balancing the essential amino acids by using proper food combinations. For example, legumes that are abundant in lysine are deficient in methionine and should be eaten with cereal grains that contain methionine but are poor in lysine.

The Zen macrobiotic diet is a rigid system which gradually eliminates animal products, vegetables, and fruits. The "highest" of ten stages of restriction are nutritionally inadequate and dangerous to the growth and health of children. Strict adherence to the most rigid diets can lead to many nutritional deficiency disorders and even death.

One benefit of the vegetarian diet is decreased calories with increased fiber, contributing to less obesity and lower serum cholesterol.

When an infant is weaned and throughout the growing years, it is difficult to provide adequate calcium, riboflavin, and vitamins D and B_{12} without dairy foods and other animal foods, from which vitamin B_{12} is derived.

REFERENCES

Carson, J.A.S., and Gorman, A. (1976). *Disease-medication relationships in altered taste sensitivity.* American Dietetic Association, *68*, 550.

Cleveland, J.O., and Berkowitz, A.J. (1975). *Educational implications in medical problems in the classroom.* Chicago: Charles C. Thomas.

Committee on Nutritional Misinformation (1975). *Hazards of overuse of vitamin D.* American Journal of Clinical Nutrition, *28*, 512.

Foltz, E.E., Barboska, C.J. and Ivy, A.C. (1944). *The level of vitamin B complex in the diet at which detectable symptoms of deficiency occur in man.* Gastroenterology, *2*, 323.

Goodhart, R.S., and Shils, M.E. (1973). *Modern Nutrition in health and disease.* Philadelphia: Lea & Febinger, p. 718.

Grande, F., Anderson, J.T., and Keys, A. (1958). *Changes of basal metabolic rate in man in semi-starvation and refeeding.* Journal of Applied Physiology, *12*, 230.

Rhead, W.J., and Schrauzer, G.N. (1971). *Risks of long-term ascorbic acid overdosage.* Nutrition Reviews, *29*, 262.

Stedman's Medical Dictionary (1976). Baltimore: Williams & Wilkins, p. 1346.

BIBLIOGRAPHY
ON
DRUG–NUTRIENT INTERACTIONS

Carr, C.J. (1982). *Food and drug interactions.* Annual Review of Pharmacology and Toxicology, *22*, 19-29.

Griffin, J.P. (1981). *Drug interactions occurring during absorption from the gastrointestinal tract.* Pharmacology and Therapeutics, *15*, 79-88.

Hamilton, C.H., and Bidlack, W.R. (1984). *Dietary concerns associated with the use of medications.* Journal of the American Dietetic Association, *84*, 901-914.

Long, J.W. (1984). *Clinical management of prescription drugs.* Philadelphia: Harper & Row.

Martin, D.W., Mayes, P.A., and Rodwell, V.W. (1983). *Harper's review of biochemistry.* Los Altos, CA: Lange Medical Publishers.

Matsui, M.S., and Rozovski, S.J. (1982). *Drug-nutrient interactions.* Clinical Therapeutics, *4*, 423-440.

Roe, D.A. (1983). *Drug and nutrient interactions.* In, H.A. Schneider (Ed.) Nutritional support of medical practice. Philadelphia: Harper & Row.

Smith, C.H., and Bidlack, W.R. (1982). *Food and drug interactions.* Food Technology, 99-103.

CHAPTER 3

Evaluation of the Nutritional Status of the Handicapped Child

Iris M. Crump

Teachers, nurses, and therapists are traditionally trained to be excellent observers, and will frequently question a behavior or appearance that suggests a nutritional problem. A child may be alternately listless or irritable; he or she may have spongy, bleeding gums or thin, brittle hair, the child may be underweight and short in stature. These, and other clinical signs of poor nutritional status, are listed in Table 1–5, to alert the school staff to needs for nutrition evaluation.

Again, the development of poor eating behavior is a problem encountered frequently among students in special education programs. For example, a child with cerebral palsy may have structural or functional damage of the oral mechanism. Spasticity can deter the development of chewing and swallowing, and special training is often required. Chapters 4 and 5 discuss many of the problems school staffs need to address to improve the oral function of these students. Adequate nutriture and speech development are the goals of individual education programs for feeding training. If nutrition goals are ignored, delayed growth, weight loss, and poor health may occur. In addition, the child may continue to accept only smooth, cooked foods and thereby miss the pleasure of tasting a wide variety of solid foods.

SCREENING DIETARY INTAKE

In addition to nutritional factors that contribute to a student's health, genetic, medical, and environmental factors may also be involved. When a child's health status is questioned, the school nurse or nurse-aide typically make inquiries and do periodic checks of the condition described. An observation of the child's eating behavior will provide some clues to disorders of appetite, food preferences, or oral function. As part of an asessment, food records can be kept for 3 days both at home and at school. Keeping records for 2 week-days plus a weekend's food intake will give a representative picture, if meals and snacks are typical and the reporting is accurate. A brief page of instructions on recording food eaten and a food diary form are shown in Figures 3–1 and 3–2. A telephone call or letter to the parents should precede the request for food records so that parents understand the teacher's concern and do not feel threatened; they are often grateful for help when a feeding problem or nutritional concern exists. The nurse or teacher can summarize a child's intake and compare it to the size and number of servings of the five basic food groups recommended for the child's age, as were suggested in Chapter 1.

Food groups are not adequate for evaluation of each nutrient consumed, but can reveal glaring omissions or excesses. For example, a child may be eating no foods in the milk group and have an excessive intake from the bread and cereal group. Dislike for milk could be a reason, but using adequate amounts of other dairy products and foods containing fresh or nonfat powdered milk can supply the nutrients the child lacks. Deviations from the recommended pattern should be discussed with the family; however, if a family believes that dairy products increase mucous secretion in their child's throat, dairy products will be withheld. The principal sources of essential calcium, riboflavin, and vitamin D are consequently omitted, as well as important supplies of calories, protein, B complex vitamins, and many minerals. As a result of these nutrient deficiencies, osteoporosis (demineralization of bone) can contribute to bone fractures, as well as a decrease in the healthy function of nerves, eyes, and skin. The damage is not readily identified, but poses insidious threats to the child's health

Figure 3—1. Instructions for keeping a 24-hour food record.

NAME: _____

DATE: _____

Please write down all food and beverages your child consumes at home for three days: Thursday, Friday, and Saturday. Do not plan for special foods; we want to know what is normally eaten. Please include any vitamins-mineral supplements or medications that are given regularly. Record the date, time, and amount for a full 24-hour day. We will also record what your child eats and drinks at school. Show the amount actually eaten, not how much was put in the dish.

Use measuring cups or spoons to describe the amount. For example:

1 cup Cheerios
1/2 cup milk (whole)
1 tsp sugar

For pieces of food that do not fit in a cup or spoon, write down the size. For example:

1 tortilla (6 inches across)
1 piece cheese (3 inches square, ¼ inch thick)

Tell what is in a mixed food. For example: 1 cup stew (¼ cup meat, ¼ cup potatoes, ¼ cup carrots, ¼ cup gravy).

Describe preparation method. For example:

1 chicken leg (fried in Crisco, no flour or batter)

Remember the little things like butter, jelly, sugar, gravy, or salad dressing.

Do not write in the spaces on the right hand side of the sheet.

If the dates are not convenient, please call me.

Please return the records to school with your child on Monday. We will call you to arrange a time to discuss them.

Thank you,

Telephone:

Figure 3–2. 24-Hour Food Record.

Date & Time	Quantity	ALL FOODS AND BEVERAGES	FOOD GROUPS # OF SERVINGS				
			Fruits & Vegetables	Bread & Cereals	Dairy Products	Meat & Alternates	Other
		Total ☐☐					
		Recommended ☐☐					

Height_____
Weight_____

Name_____
Birth Date_____

Was this a typical day?_____ If not, why?_____

Vitamin supplement?_____ Quantity_____ Hours sleep_____
Mineral or other supplement?_____ _____ Hours sitting_____
Medication?_____ _____ Hours active_____

(Krause and Mahan, 1984). Poor growth, posture, and dentition are clues to the damage, with x-ray verifying bone demineralization. A dietitian experienced in treating the dietary problems of children should be consulted.

Function of the Dietitian

In addition to clarification of quantity and preparation methods of foods, the dietitian can collect a nutritional history to examine use of special preparations, medications, vitamin and mineral or other supplements, as well as the cultural and personal food preferences (Meritt and Blackburn, 1981). The dietitian can calculate the individual nutrients total and help the family to provide all essential nutrients using methods the child can accept and be able to eat, with consideration to his present level of oral development. The dietitian can then advise the school staff and parents of the appropriate uses of the milk group to assure no disturbance of function, and may also prescribe alternate foods or supplements with the approval of the child's physician. This will avoid any dispute between school and home concerning appropriate feeding of the child.

The dietitian can discuss with a physician the specific studies or routine laboratory screening that will indicate whether there is a need for further study of a student's nutritional status (Yip, Schwartz, and Deinard, 1983), such as that for the child who drinks milk only, and omits most other foods, or who takes anticonvulsants that interfere with vitamin D metabolism (Roe, 1976). Follow-up of this nature is often the result of school staff's alertness to both the clinical signs of malnutrition and a search for its cause.

ANTHROPOMETRIC MEASUREMENTS

Physical growth in mentally retarded individuals was first studied by Tarbell in 1883. The correlation between anthropometry and intellect was hypothesized, with further studies suggesting a positive correlation between mental defect and growth failure. However, marked variation between individuals exists, and generalizations should not be made. The value of the studies is in their promotion of further investigation of factors contributing to abnormal mental and physical growth, including pre- and postnatal malnutrition. Genetic influences are summarized in Chapter 5 and endocrine and neurophysiological influences are reported in Chapter 6.

Pryor and Thelander (1967) concluded that children with Down syndrome demonstrate shortness of stature due to shortening of the lower extremities. It was also shown in their investigation that multiple congenital anomalies not due to chromosomal aberration were accompanied by poor growth. Cerebral palsy from birth injury affected children's growth adversely to a lesser degree that defects originating prenatally. Mild hypoxia at birth, however, showed no influence on growth.

Methods of Growth Measurement

In this section we will use the longitudinal record of an individual's growth to anticipate caloric and nutrient needs. By plotting the individual child's growth pattern, the adequacy of his or her food intake is reflected in that individual's growth rate rather than in the height of the average child of the same age. For example, a child's height may be genetically determined to remain at the fifth percentile of children that age, by consecutive measurements showing continued growth at the same percentile. A drop in height and weight below that individual's growth curve indicates a need for monitoring the child's food intake and other conditions that might be contributing to the decrease in growth rate.

Equipment and materials needed for accurate measurement of growth include the following:

1. National Center for Health Statistics (NCHS) growth charts, available from pharmaceutical and formula companies. Examples are seen in Figures 3–3 and 3–4.
2. A balance scale, checked regularly for accuracy.
3. Two plastic or metal tape measures-one for recumbent (lying down) length for the nonambulatory child, the other that fastens to a wall for standing height.
4. A packet of disposable tape measures for measurement of head circumference.
5. Optional: calipers for skinfold measurement.

The most reliable prediction of the energy needs of children with Down syndrome, as well as other growth defects, is the height of the child, rather than age (Cully, 1965). To obtain the height-age, measure horizontally on the growth graph (Figure 3–3) to the 50th percentile at the child's height, and mark it; then measure laterally to the age at that height and mark it. Figure 3–3 describes Ted, a 7-year-old boy with spastic cerebral palsy who is 43 inches in height. This places him at the 5-year height-age. Table 3–1 gives averages of the energy (calorie) needs of children as advised

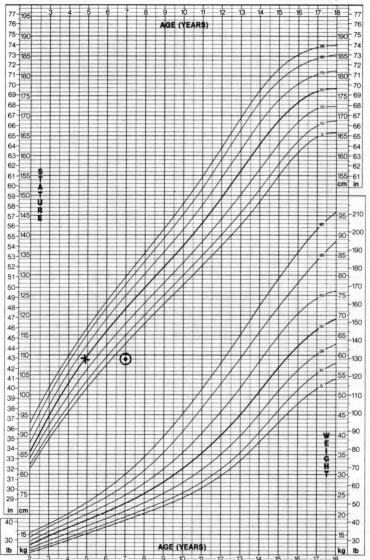

Figure 3-3. Boys: prepubescent physical growth NCHS percentiles. Adapted from Hamill, P.V.V., Drizd, T.A., Johnson, C.L., Reed, R.B., Roche, A.F., Moore, W.M. Physical growth: National Center for Health Statistics percentiles. American Journal of Clinical Nutrition 32: 607-629, 1979. Data from the National Center for Health Statistics (NCHS), Hyattsville, MD. Provided as a service of Ross Laboratories, © 1980.

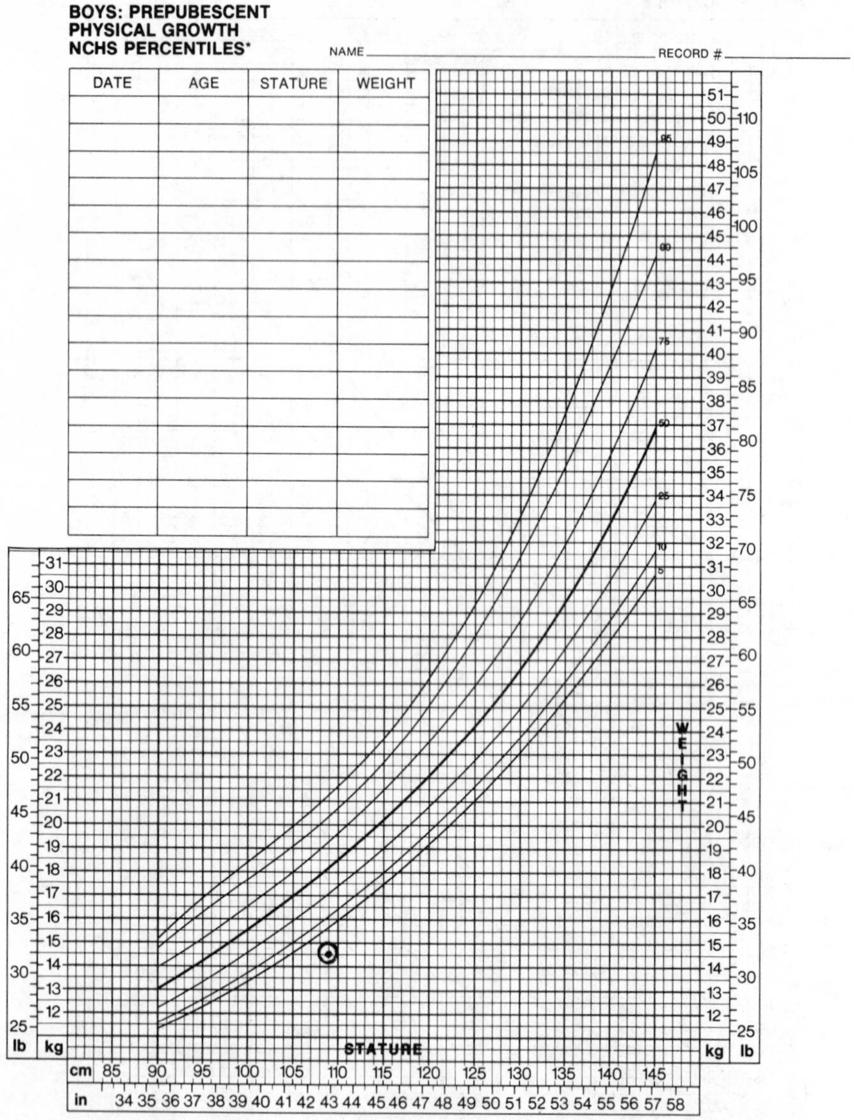

BOYS: PREPUBESCENT PHYSICAL GROWTH NCHS PERCENTILES

Figure 3-4. Boys: prepubescent physical growth NCHS percentiles. Adapted from Hamill, P.V.V., Drizd, T.A., Johnson, C.L., Reed, R.B., Roche, A.F., Moore, W.M.: Physical growth: National Center for Health Statistics percentiles. American Journal of Clinical Nutrition 32: 607-629, 1979. Data from the National Center for Health Statistics (NCHS), Hyattsville, MD. c 1980 Ross Laboratories.

Table 3–1. Recommended Energy Intakes for Children of Various Ages

	Age	Weight (kg)	(lb)	Height (cm)	(in.)	Energy needs (kcal)	Range
Infants	0.0–0.5	6	13	60	24	kg × 115	(95–145)
	0.5–1.0	9	20	71	28	kg × 105	(80–135)
Children	1–3	13	29	90	35	1300	(900–1800)
	4–6	20	44	112	44	1700	(1300–2300)
	7–10	28	62	132	52	2400	(1650–3300)
Males	11–14	45	99	157	62	2700	(2000–3700)
	15–18	66	145	176	69	2800	(2100–3900)
Females	11–14	46	101	157	62	2200	(1500–3000)
	15–18	55	120	163	64	2100	(1200–3000)

From *Food and Nutrition Board: Recommended dietary allowances,* (rev. ed. 9) 1980, Washington, D.C.; National Academy of Sciences, National Research Council.

by the National Research Council of the National Academy of Sciences and stated in the publication, *Recommended dietary allowances (RDA),* 1980.

The adjusted RDA predicts that an energy intake of 1700 kilocalories is needed for Ted's height-age, as compared to 2400 kilocalories recommended based on his chronological age.

On the weight-for-length growth grid (Figure 3–4), less than the 25th or more than the 75th percentile indicates a need for nutrition consultation. This places Ted below the 5th percentile, and indicates an urgent need for nutritional intervention.

Children with cerebral palsy and a decreased activity level use only 10 kcal/cm of height, while those with normal or increased levels require 15 kcal/cm of height (Berg and Isaksson, 1970). The child's food intake may not supply the calories appropriate for his or her activity level. Therefore, it is important that growth charts be kept for children who show sharp deviations or gradual but continuing shifts from one percentile position to another (Fiser, Meredith, and Elders, 1975). The school nurse can contact the family, physician, and dietitian to investigate the cause of change in linear growth velocity or weight gain. Sequential measurements will show a change in rate of gain, which is an important indicator of nutritional status, as are other anthropometric indices.

In some schools, the physical education instructor or nurse will use calipers to measure the triceps skinfold and arm and chest circumference. Tables are then used to compare the individual's measurements to averages, as is explained in the chapter on Nutritional Assessment in the *Manual of Pediatric Nutrition* (Ney, 1984). Head circumference should correspond in size to the child's length and should be reported if it falls below the child's growth curve in sequential measurements.

LABORATORY INDICES OF NUTRITIONAL DEFICIENCIES

Utilization of nutrients may be affected by drugs or physiological deficits. While tests can be done if specific deficiencies are suspected, a nutritional screen is more cost effective. A complete blood count with differential, serum albumin, and urinalysis can reveal many types of malnutrition. When malnutrition is found, the student's physician or health-care provider should be alerted to the teacher's and nurse's concern. When possible, a report should be made to the nurse to establish corrective feeding or medication prescribed.

A supplement of specific vitamins and minerals will often treat a deficiency while eating habits are undergoing change. The dietitian and the nurse or nurse's aide will work with the teaching staff to ensure that the food the child eats provides the calories and protein recommended. Until the child's oral skills and acceptance of a variety of foods improves, the supplement will supply missing nutrients. When all of the nutrients needed are supplied by improved food intake, the supplement should be discontinued.

REFERENCES

Berg, K, and Isaksson, G. (1970). Body composition and nutrition of school children with cerebral palsy. *Acta Paediatrica Scandinavia, 205*, 41.

Cully, W.J., Goyal, K., Jolly, D.H., and Merty, E.T. (1965). Caloric intake of children with Down syndrome. *Journal of Pediatrics. 66*, 772.

Fiser, R.H. Jr., Meredith, P.D. and Elders, J.M. (1975). The child who fails to grow. *American Family Physician*, (II), *6*, 108.

Krause, M.V. and Mahan, L.K. (1984). *Food, nutrition and diet therapy* (p. 296). Philadelphia: W.B. Saunders.

Meritt, R.J., Blackburn, G.L. (1981). Nutritional assessment and metabolic response to illness of the hospitalized child. In R. Suskind (Ed.), *Textbook of pediatric nutrition* (p. 296). New York: Raven Press.

Ney, D.M. (1984). Nutritional assessment. In D.G. Kelts et al. (Eds.), *Manual of pediatric nutrition.* (pp. 107–116). Boston: Little, Brown.

Pryor, H.B., Thelander, H.E. (1967). Growth deviations in handicapped children. *Clinical Pediatrics 6,* (No. 8), 501.

Roe, D.A. (1976). *Drug induced nutritional deficiencies* (pp. 54, 211). Westport, CN: AVI Publishing Co.

Tarbell, G.G. (1883). On the height, weight and relative growth of normal and feeble-minded children. *Proceedings of the Association of Medical Officers, American Institute for Idiotic and Feeble-Minded Persons 1,* 188.

Yip, R., Schwartz, S., and Deinard, A.S. (1983). Screening for iron deficiency with the erythrocyte protoporphyrin test, *Pediatrics, 72,* 214-219.

CHAPTER 4

Identification, Evaluation, and Management of Feeding Disorders

Amy G. Salomon
Cornelia Lieb-Lundell

The child's ability to learn effectively is created by physical, sensory, and communicative environments. The child is constantly exposed to multisensory information that includes vision, hearing, taste, smell, touch, movement, and pressure. Depending on the child's state of receptivity to incoming information, input will be attended to and processed, or it may need to be filtered out as distracting or not essential to learning (Morris, 1982).

Children with developmental disabilities have difficulties integrating all necessary information from their physical, sensory, and communicative environments. Information can be perceived as confusing, noxious, nondescript, or nonmeaningful in relation to their unique and individual system. A child with cerebral palsy may exhibit increased muscle tone around the face, lips, and tongue; this makes physical mobility for handling food difficult. Sensory information received from a bite of hamburger, for example, could send the message "what do I do with all these little pieces that are in my mouth?:" the result is frequently the child's spitting out, choking, passively swallowing, or having pieces of food lodged in various places within the mouth or throat. More frequently than not, the result of "distorted" sensory input will take the form of learned, compensatory responses created by the child for survival, as well as for communication.

For the nonverbal child, or the one who has significant delays in expressive language and feeding skills, the method of communication will take the form of a behavior the child has creatively adopted. Often these behaviors, such as spitting food up or out, pushing food away, crying or screaming, or turning away with averted eye gaze, are considered socially inappropriate, harmful to the self and to others. It is imperative that all therapists and teachers first accept these behaviors as the child's unique and creative attempts to communicate information they cannot otherwise express. The role of facilitators of learning is to actively explore with the child what is being communicated in relation to sensory and physical environments. Once this has been done, the goal becomes to provide the child with opportunities to create more meaningful, appropriate responses within a positive learning environment.

FEEDING ENVIRONMENT

When looking at the feeding process, we can appreciate the interaction of many aspects of the child's world. Figure 4–1 attempts to represent the unbroken circle in interaction: Inside the circle, areas of feeding, speech, and sensory modalities are viewed as interdependent with one another. Looking at the relationship between feeding skills and speech, one might view the feeding process as a frequent frame of reference for the child to experience and practice various movement patterns, sensory reception, perception, and discrimination skills connected to speech.

Along the outside of the circle are other areas that impact on the feeding process. Aspects of nutrition have been addressed earlier. The child's readiness skills, including underlying cognitive abilities, receptive language, and ability to create responses certainly are important to the feeding process. All children, regardless of the degree of their disability, will process some information that is unique and meaningful to them. A child who is mildly affected with cerebral palsy, for example, who comprehends what is said, can actively make choices as to what and when he or she

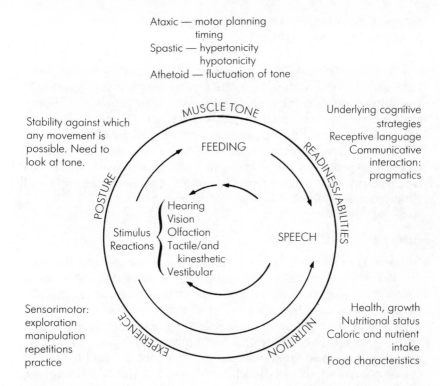

Ataxic — motor planning
timing
Spastic — hypertonicity
hypotonicity
Athetoid — fluctuation of tone

MUSCLE TONE

Stability against which
any movement is
possible. Need to
look at tone.

FEEDING

POSTURE

Stimulus
Reactions

Hearing
Vision
Olfaction
Tactile/and
kinesthetic
Vestibular

SPEECH

READINESS/ABILITIES

Underlying cognitive
strategies
Receptive language
Communicative
interaction:
pragmatics

Sensorimotor:
exploration
manipulation
repetitions
practice

EXPERIENCE

NUTRITION

Health, growth
Nutritional status
Caloric and nutrient
intake
Food characteristics

Figure 4–1. The unbroken circle of interaction: Areas of feeding, speech, and
sensory modalities are interdependent with one another.

wants to eat. Such a child will present different behaviors than
the child who is being tube fed, is blind, deaf, or whose physical
difficulties limit most purposeful movement.

The child's sensory motor experiences within the environment
also influence the feeding process. Just as feeding provides the
child with opportunities to practice oral motor movements necessary for speech production, the opportunities for motoric exploration, repetitive movement patterns, and transitions from one
movement to another, provide a rich variety of sensory motor
experiences for the child. These experiences are naturally rein-
forced by the parents and other people in the environment. The
child who is limited motorically, experiences difficulties with active
exploration of each environment. This can affect the messages
the child perceives and, thus, what is experienced.

NORMAL DEVELOPMENT OF ORAL MOTOR STRUCTURES AND FEEDING SKILLS

In many abnormally developing infants, early feeding problems are the first signs of an already present but only gradually emerging disability. Further, these early feeding problems in many children may persist far beyond infancy and therefore interfere with the ability to develop age-appropriate feeding skills.

Normal development is the foundation for both assessment of feeding problems and development of intervention plans. To understand the normal, one must consider both the anatomy and functional development of the oral cavity.

Anatomy of the Oral Cavity

The combination of the oral and nasal cavity and the oral tract can be viewed as a continuous tube: it contains a series of valves that work to direct food once it has entered the mouth. These valves are the various structures of the entire oral-pharyngeal mechanism (Morris, 1982). It is helpful to know that the oral structure undergoes a developmental progression just as oral function does. When we compare the mouth and pharynx of the newborn with that of the adult (Figures 4–2 and 4–3) we can see that the position of the various structures changes with maturation. These changes actually occur within the first 2 years of life.

Functionally, these anatomical relationships provide the newborn and very young child with inborn stability. The purpose of that stability is to make swallowing easier and protect the airway. In the older child or adult, stability yields to mobility and the increasing coordination of the oral structures eliminates the need for the previous stability.

When feeding problems are suspected or identified in a child, evaluation should begin with an assessment i.e., visual inspection, of oral structures, the purpose of which is to rule out any structural abnormalities that may influence feeding behavior.

Development of Feeding Skills

In general, feeding development occurs in a predictable and systematic manner. Some useful normal developmental milestones related to feeding can be found in Table 4–1. A brief review of some major feeding patterns of the infant that are the basis of later feeding skills are herewith described.

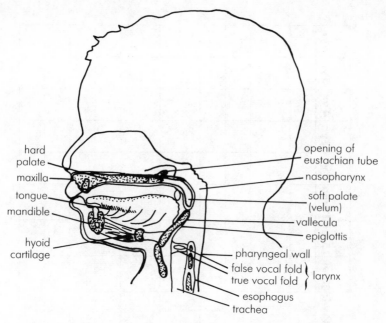

Figure 4–2. The mouth and pharynx of the newborn (saggital section).

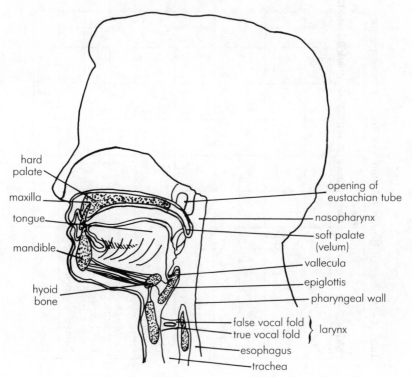

Figure 4–3. The mouth and pharynx of the adult (saggital section).

Table 4–1. Selected Normal Milestones of Feeding Development

Skill	New-born	12 wk	20 wk	26 wk	32 wk	36 wk	40 wk	44 wk	48 wk	15 mo	18 mo	2 yr	3 yr	4 yr	5 yr	6 yr
Suckle-swallow	+	+														
Vertical chewing movement of tongue			+													
True suck begins				+												
Coordinated swallow				+												
Tongue moves food side-to-side					+											
Good lip closure over spoon					+											
Rotary chewing						+										
Feeds self cracker							+									
Drinks from cup (assist)								+								
Finger feeds									+							

Skill	New-born	12 wk	20 wk	26 wk	32 wk	36 wk	40 wk	44 wk	48 wk	15 mo	18 mo	2 yr	3 yr	4 yr	5 yr	6 yr
Cup holds—1 or 2 hands										+						
Spoon, cannot fill spills, turns at mouth											+					
Spoon, fills overhand grasp, no turn												+				
Combined feeding finger, spoon, fork													+			
Spoon—uses well														+		
Drinks with straw														+		
Fork—uses															+	
Knife—uses															+	
Eat and talk combined															+	
Assists with table set																+

From *Nutrition and Feeding of the Handicapped Child*, by Iris M. Crump. © 1987 by College-Hill Press, a division of Little, Brown, and Company, Inc. Reproduction of this material for any purpose other than clinical work or training is prohibited.

Sucking is basic to survival in the newborn. Initially, we look to see that sucking motions are efficient with good lip closure, minimal loss of liquid, and good coordination of sucking, swallowing, and breathing. The suck has several developmental stages. Briefly defined, they are:

1. The lips are closed and the tongue and jaw engage in rhythmical pressure against the nipple.
2. The baby progresses to forward-back movements of the tongue on the nipple.
3. The final stage is a controlled up-and-down movement of the tongue on the nipple.

Cup drinking begins with the child attempting to "suck" on the edge of a cup with a great deal of stability. This gradually changes to a sipping as lip action increases and mobility replaces stability in oral motor function. In the older child, who is not holding a cup independently, the feeder frequently places the cup too far into the child's mouth. This position only encourages the child to continue to use the cup edge as a support surface.

Using a *spoon,* as with a cup, the baby initially uses a sucking pattern to take food off the spoon. (Incidentally, many mothers just "dump" the spoonful into the baby's mouth and do not wait for the baby's participation.) More mature patterns begin to develop as soon as coordinated function appears; the baby begins to remove food from the spoon and creates a bolus (mass) in the mouth. This bolus is then sent to the back of the oral cavity to be swallowed once the entrance to the airway is closed.

Biting and chewing progression usually begins with straight up-and-down movements of the jaw. This is replaced with an anterior–posterior (forward–back) motion of the jaw and tongue, and finally a rotary component emerges. During this progression, the child also begins to activate independent tongue motions for the purpose of moving food to the side of the mouth. The key concept here is the gradual development of coordinated movements that are no longer part of the total patterns previously observed.

Finger feeding to self-feeding also has a clearly defined progression:

1. When the child begins to eat solids, he or she will attempt to push food into the mouth from the palm of the hand.
2. With increased skill, the movement of placing food in the mouth with the fingertips begins.

3. The child will master cup drinking and spoon feeding (with spills) by about 18 to 21 months.
4. The 2-year-old has mastered basic spoon feeding, but with an overhand grasp of the spoon.

Once the child has mastered the basic finger and spoon feeding skills, more mature abilities gradually develop. Over the next several years the child will learn to use a fork and knife and finally attain basic table manners by about age 6.

POSITIONING THE CHILD FOR FEEDING

When feeding problems are suspected or identified, a primary area of concern should be posture and position used in assisted- or self-feeding (Figure 4–4). Problem areas to be considered are postural alignment and head control.

Whether in the classroom or at home, an appropriate chair or seating device should be identified for each child. In some cases, consultation with a physical or occupational therapist may be helpful. In general, the child should be seated in an upright position for eating. While it is true that the very young child is fed in a semi-reclining position in the parent's lap, this position should not be perpetuated with the older child.

The basic position of the child seated at the table allows the feet to be placed flat and supported, the hips and knees at a right angle, and the back straight and supported against the chair. The table height should allow the elbow and forearm to be placed on the table at an approximate right angle to the shoulder. The question of table and chair height for each child will need to be considered in relation to the total eating environment. When children are small, it may be appropriate to lower the chair and table height to allow them to place their feet on the floor. In the home environment, children may be more appropriately raised to a customary table height so as to fit into the family as a whole for the mealtime.

Two areas requiring careful management in preparing for feeding are the head and hip positions. In many children with central nervous system disorders, the head position governs the distribution of muscle tone throughout the body. For the child who is fed in a semi-reclined position with the head pulled back, active manipulation of the food in the mouth cannot develop and the child comes to rely on gravity for swallowing.

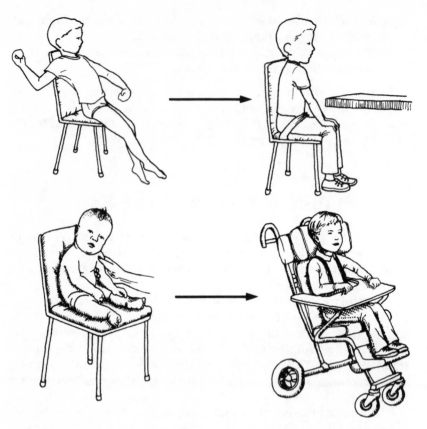

Figure 4—4. Correction of positioning problems in preparation for feeding.

When the hip position is carefully controlled, it will provide the child a stable base. For sitting, the child's hips should be positioned securely on the chair with equal distribution of weight, and the trunk should be directly positioned over the hips. When support straps are used, these should always be directed over the pelvis and not be allowed to ride up over the child's abdomen.

EQUIPMENT AND SPECIAL UTENSILS

Careful selection and use of feeding equipment or utensils may help to advance the child's feeding skills and overcome some problems related to individual handicapping conditions. Items appropriate for the individual child may be supplied by the family or purchased by the school. There are a variety of commercial resources for equipment, some of which are listed at the end of this chapter, in Appendix 4–1. Before choosing any type of specialized adaptive device, an attempt should be made to use or to adapt regular utensils.

Using regular or, if necessary, minimally adapted utensils has several advantages: first, it reaffirms the normal aspects of the child for the family and others; second, when special equipment is not available, it allows the child to participate fully in meals without being limited; finally, it helps to minimize the complexity of caring for a child who may have other specialized needs.

When adapted utensils are necessary, some specific considerations in choosing equipment are:

1. Appropriateness to the child's development, as well as chronological age.
2. Practical, easy to clean, and keep clean.
3. Not prohibitively expensive and possible to replace if lost or broken.
4. In the classroom, consistent with other classroom equipment to as much of an extent possible.

Once a decision has been made to use specialized utensils with a child, careful attention must be given to meeting the child's individual needs. Some examples follow.

Cup drinking may present special problems. Prior to cup drinking, the child may have already had difficulties holding a bottle. In some cases, a child can handle a 4-ounce plastic bottle or divided bottle, but not the standard 8-ounce bottle. Once the child progresses to a cup, poor motor control may lead to frequent spilling. A spouted or weighted cup can be helpful in this situation. The spouted cup, as well as the "cut-out" cup, will help the child who cannot sufficiently tilt the head back (Figure 4–5).

Figure 4–5. Examples of modified drinking cups and bottle for the handicapped child.

For the child with a poor grasp, some form of built-up handle for eating utensils may be appropriate and could be achieved by wrapping a handle with tape, slipping a handle into a plastic tube, such as a foam hair curler or foam tubing commonly found in hardware stores, or purchasing one of a variety of plastic-handle spoons. Latex-coated spoons may protect the child's gum from injury when a bite reflex is present (Figure 4–6).

Placing or scooping food onto a spoon or fork may present a particular problem for the handicapped child with decreased control or coordination. A bowl or plate with a raised edge or "lip" may help his problem by giving the child a solid surface upon which to push food. In some cases, divided dishes serve the same purpose and also help to maintain and separate different colors, textures, and tastes of food (Figure 4–7).

Beyond providing adaptive utensils, the child's usual feeding environment can be altered. When there is a problem keeping the plate stationary, and a suction cup is not practical, a wet washcloth, an "octopus" soap holder, or piece of Grippistrip or Dycem under the plate will create a nonslip surface. For some children, raising the plate will help decrease spilling or misdirecting

Figure 4–6. Examples of modified eating utensils for the handicapped child.

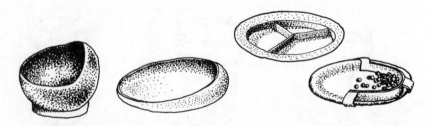

Figure 4–7. Examples of scoop bowls and special plates for the handicapped child.

the spoon by shortening the distance from scooping the food to placing it in the mouth.

The potential for adapting the feeding environment is infinite. The classroom teacher should, however, try to focus on the goal of normalizing the feeding situation to as much an extent possible. Basic guidelines to achieving this are: (1) to balance the child's individual needs with the overall classroom expectation; (2) to progress from choosing simple to increasingly adaptive equipment in solving problems; (3) to use approaches that work in multiple settings and allow the child maximum exposure to one method; and (4) to continuously re-evaluate the situation and attempt to introduce a higher skill level.

ASSESSMENT OF FEEDING SKILLS

Frequently, the classroom teacher will observe a child's feeding behaviors that could be of concern. Some of these behaviors could warrant further investigation by a feeding team, typically consisting of a physical therapist, occupational therapist, speech therapist, and nutritionist. Ideally, the classroom teacher and the child's primary therapists are invited to participate. The parents may also attend, or should be given a summary of the team's recommendations when they do not attend.

The presence of any of the following behaviors may be indicative of a feeding disorder:

1. Drools profusely
2. Pushes food out with tongue
3. Cannot swallow in an upright position
4. Gags or vomits frequently when eating
5. Will not tolerate a spoon or cup near the mouth
6. Does not chew
7. Refuses to take liquids from a cup or glass
8. Cannot or refuses to finger feed
9. Cannot or refuses to self-feed with a utensil
10. Is not eating a food consistency that is appropriate his or her age level
11. Appears to be selective about which foods to eat or refuses to eat certain foods

Once the teacher has identified a potential feeding problem, a full team evaluation may be necessary. There are many feeding clinic evaluation forms available, some of which are listed in Appendix 4–2. The following information needs to be provided through such an evaluation by an interdisciplinary team.

Areas Covered During Feeding Assessment

ANATOMICAL STRUCTURE AND CONDITION OF THE ORAL PHARYNGEAL CAVITY. Evaluation generally begins with a brief review of the child's physical characteristics with specific attention to the oral area. Since height and weight measurements should be done with the child undressed, they may be deferred until the end of the evaluation process. Assessment for dental development should include the following:

- Bite
- Teeth
- Gums
- Dental hygiene

Physical condition of the child is evaluated; including

- Height
- Weight
- Skin color

POSITIONING. The basic concept of good positioning was presented earlier in this chapter. At the beginning of the evaluation, the parent is asked to demonstrate the position usually used for feeding. When this position appears inadequate or inappropriate, an attempt to modify it may be made.

POSTURAL ASSESSMENT AND ORAL REFLEXES. The examination usually begins with a systematic evaluation of general function. Postural function as related to feeding includes assessment of the following:

- Head and trunk control
- Overall posture
- General muscle tone
- Limitations of movement

Motor-control assessment for hand function would include these items:

- Reflex activity
- Eye-hand coordination
- Patterns of grasp
- Volitional control and function using utensils

Oral reflex assessments include the following:

- Rooting
- Suck/swallow
- Bite
- Gag

ORAL PHARYNGEAL FUNCTION AT REST AND DURING SPONTANEOUS FUNCTION. This is an observational state of the evaluation that provides background information about the child's function prior to observation of the actual feeding process. Specific functional areas to observe include:

- Jaw
- Lips
- Tongue

FEEDING BEHAVIOR. At this point the parent may be asked to demonstrate how the child is usually fed or allowed to eat. Various components of feeding are observed. In some cases the parent may be asked to attempt a different procedure, or a team member may take over a portion of the feeding. The parent is asked to feed the child a food that he or she can handle and one that cannot be handled. The following specific functions are assessed:

- Sucking/drinking
- Swallowing
- Chewing

COMMUNICATION: RESPIRATION, PHONATION, RESONANCE, ARTICULATION. The child's process of communicating and understanding communication is observed throughout the evaluation. Parents are also asked to share with the team information on how the child communicates in various settings. Assessments include:

- Breathing patterns
- Voice (pitch, volume, intonation)
- Non-oral system of communication
- Speech (fluency, articulation)
- Language comprehension and expression

SUMMARY. The purpose of the summary is to list those observations the will be used to develop a plan of intervention. The summary should therefore contain key issues related to the child's problem(s). Key summary items include:

- Description of mealtime interaction
- Assets
- Liabilities

GOALS AND TREATMENT PLAN. Ideally, this section contains a specific plan of action that is time-limited and goal-oriented, and includes recommendations and follow-up plan.

SUMMARY

In order for a feeding program to be successful for any child, it is imperative that goals and recommendations are structured so that they can be addressed by school, therapy, and home programs. Consistency, communication among programs, and follow-up are necessary aspects of the child's feeding program. Special attention should be given to sensory, physical, and communicative environments and how each can affect the mealtime experience. The ability to observe, assess, and make necessary adjustments creates the potential for developing new feeding skills for the child.

REFERENCE

Morris, S.E. (1982). *The normal acquisition of oral feeding skills: Implications for assessment and treatment.* Central Islip, NY: Therapeutic Media, Inc.

BIBLIOGRAPHY

Ardrian, G.M., and Kemp, F.H. (1970). Some important factors in the assessment of oro-pharyngeal function. *Developmental Medicine and Child Neurology 12,* 158-166.

Davis, L.F. (1979). Pre-speech. In Connor, G. Williamson and J. Siep (Eds.), *Program guidelines for infants and toddlers with neuro-motor and other developmental disabilities.* New York: Teachers College Press.

Feeding Clinic Orientation: *Manual* (1979). Los Angeles, CA: University Affiliated Program, Children's Hospital of Los Angeles.

Finnie, N.R. (1975). *Handling the young cerebral palsied child at home.* (2nd ed.). New York: E.P. Dutton.

Gunther, M., and Toftgruben, J. (1982). *School nutrition and food service techniques.* California State Department of Education: Office of Child Nutrition Services.

Ingram, T.T.S. (1967). Clinical significance of the infantile feeding reflexes. *Developmental Medicine and Child Neurology 4,* 159-169.

McClannahan, C. (1985). *Feeding and caring for infants and children with special needs.* St. Paul, Minn: Gillette Children's Hospital,

Morris, S.E. (1977). *Program guidelines for children with feeding problems.* Edison, N.J: Childcraft Education Corp.

Smith, M.J. (19). *Feeding the handicapped child.* Memphis, TN: University of Tennessee,

Wilson, J.M. (Ed.). (1978). *Oral-motor function and dysfunction in children.* Chapel Hill, NC: University of North Carolina.

APPENDIX 4-1. Equipment Resource List

Achievement Products for Children, PO Box 547, Mineola, NY 11501
   Feeding equipment, specialized chairs for children

Community Playthings, Rifton, NY 12471
   Standard wooden and specialized chairs for children

ENSTE, Hitchinstrasse 36, 6530 Bingen 11, West Germany
   Feeding equipment, specialized chairs for children

Equipment Shop, PO Box 33, Bedford, MA 01730
   Wooden chairs, corner chairs for children

HASI, Friedrich Havenstein GMBH, 8000 Munich 60, Freienfeld Str. 20A,
West Germany
   Feeding equipment, specialized chairs for children

Kaymet for Cups, Etc., Mothercare for Cups and Spoons
England only — most large chemists
   Cups and spoons

G.E. Miller, Inc., 484 South Broadway, Yonkers, NY 10705
   Feeding equipment, specialized chairs for children and adults

J.A. Preston Corporation, 71 Fifth Avenue, New York, N.Y. 10003
   Feeding equipment, specialized chairs for children and adults

Fred Sammons, Inc., 145 Tower Dr., Burr Ridge, IL 60521
   Feeding equipment (utensils, plates, cups) for infants, children,
   and adults

Travenol Home Therapy/Abbey Medical (nationwide) (American Abbey
   Medical)
   Feeding equipment, specialized chairs for both children and adults

APPENDIX 4-2. Selected Feeding Assessment Forms

1. Carmen, P., and Buchberger-Frederick A. (1979). Eating Assessment Tool (Unpublished). CDMRC, University of Washington, Seattle, WA 98105.

2. Gillette Children's Hospital (1984). Feeding Assessment, 200 East University Avenue, Saint Paul, MN, 55101.

3. King-Thomas, L. (1980), UNC Feeding Assessment, University of North Carolina, Chapel Hill, NC. Adapted from Cadre Assessment Tool, Cadre Center, ISD #911, Cambridge, Minnesota, 55008.

4. Morris, S.E. (1982). Pre-speech Assessment Scale. Curative Rehabilitation Center. Distributed by J.A. Preston Corporation, 60 Page Road, Clifton, NJ, 07012.

5. San Juan Unified School District (1975). San Juan Handicapped Infant Project. San Juan Unified School District, 4848 Cottage Way, Carmichael, CA 95608.

6. Schafer, S., and M. Moersch (Eds.) (1981). Developmental Programming for Infants and Young Children. The University of Michigan Press, Ann Arbor, MI 48109.

7. University Affiliated Program (1979). Feeding Clinic Evaluation. Children's Hospital of Los Angeles, 4650 Sunset Blvd. Los Angeles, CA 90027.

CHAPTER 5

Nutrition and Congenital Disorders

Iris M. Crump

Occurrence of feeding and nutritional problems of children with handicaps that are similar follow predictable trends, and factors contributing to the problems are similar in some cases. For example, short stature and low activity level are typical of persons with Down syndrome and those having a myelomeningocele (open spine). Obesity is also prevalent in both populations, demonstrating that although etiology of the conditions differ, outcome is similar. Underweight is observed more often in children with athetoid cerebral palsy, autism, those with oral defects, or with certain syndromes, such as those described in Table 5–1. Factors that dictate both treatment and possible outcome of feeding and nutritional problems should be identified before goals and plans are decided. Some nutritional problems that appear most commonly among the school children having congenital disorders is addressed in this chapter.

DEFECTS OF THE ORAL MECHANISM

Swallowing, tongue mobility, chewing, and lip closure are affected by defects of structural (bone), myogenic (muscle), or neurological origin. Evaluation of a possible malfunction of the

Table 5–1. Eating Problems Seen in Various Syndromes

Name: Inheritance	Characteristics	Growth	Nutrition and Feeding
Down syndrome: Trisomy 21 sporadic Translocation plus mosaic heritable	Hypotonia; hyperflexibility; epicanthal eye folds; short neck with excess skin in back; small mouth; protruding tongue; slanted, small eyes, Brushfield spots; mental retardation.	Short stature due to decrease in growth of extremeties; short fiifth finger; gap between first and second toes; irregular delayed dentition.	Poor suck plus delay in development of chewing. Introduce soft table foods as soon as possible. Encourage vegetables and fruit to reduce tendency for obesity and constipation.
Prader-Willi syndrome: Fanconi syndrome: sporadic	Early hypotonia, hypogenitalism and feeding problems; usually mild mental retardation; emotional lability; upward slant of almond shaped eyes.	Delayed bone age; short stature; small hands and feet; obesity from early childhood. Fat trunk, buttocks and upper limbs.	Compulsive eating; no self-control of food intake possible; eating must be monitored. Nonketotic diabetes in adolescence without weight loss may occur. Probable low energy needs. Low-calorie diet throughout life.
Rett syndrome: sporadic: seen in females only	Severe mental retardation; early deterioration of gross motor skills. Typical hand wringing or slapping. Seizures common.	Short stature, very poor weight gain.	High fat diet (may be due to defect of carbohydrate metabolism); ketogenic diet for seizure control; frequent small meals; usually must be fed.

Name: Inheritance	Characteristics	Growth	Nutrition and Feeding
Klinefelter syndrome Extra X chromosome in at least 1 cell line	At puberty, delay in secondary sexual characteristics.	Increase in height; underweight until adolescence; increase in lower body adipose tissue.	Increase protein and fat during childhood. Decrease with adolescence. Always stress vegetables and fruit.
Cornelia de Lange syndrome	Hirsute; upturned nose; "fish shaped" mouth; mental retardation.	Failure to thrive; very small stature and abnormally small hands and feet; micrognathia and malocclusion of teeth.	Frequently tube fed in infancy; may have cleft palate; anorexia and constipation; needs optimal nutrient & caloric intake, 5 to 6 small meals, vitamin mineral supplement.
Pierre-Robin syndrome	Small mandible; cleft lip and palate; glossoptosis; defects of eyes and ears. Normal intelligence.	Normal. Surgery may repair oral defects.	May have hypotonic gag; smooth textures until retracted tongue position is corrected. Training for adaptive self-feeding helps improve self-esteem. Encourage independence.

(continued)

Table 5–1 *(continued)*

Name: Inheritance	Characteristics	Growth	Nutrition and Feeding
Lesch-Nyhan syndrome	Choreoathetosis; spasticity; mental retardation; compulsive self destructive; chewing of lips, fingers; mental regardation.	Poor growth, thin. Often megaloblastic anemia.	Soft foods, high nutrient density, frequent meals, high fluids to assist uric acid excretion; folic acid, vitamin D supplement (seizure medications disrupt their metabolism).
Rubella syndrome No inheritance.	Deafness, heart disease, cataracts, psychomotor retardation, spasticity, irritability.	Often premature, small, microcephalic.	Optimal nutrient density (see Table 6–2). Tactile defensiveness. Limits spoon feeding. Supplemental formula feedings.

oral mechanism is done by medical specialists, speech patholo-
gists, or occupational or physical therapists who have specialized
training. The nutrition consultants on the interdisciplinary team
analyze the effects of the disability on nutritional status; specific
care plans are then formulated with both school staff and parents.

In Chapter 4, assessment of feeding development and nutrient
intake was earlier described. If no extensive evaluation has been
done, however, intervention procedures as described in the section, Equipment and Special Utinsels may be appropriate.

Cleft Lip and Palate

Cleft lip and palate is a disorder of structural origin in children
who may have no other congenital defect. It appears commonly
in the child with Cornelia de Lange syndrome and is also associated with other anomalies.

PHYSIOLOGICAL DEFECT AND CORRECTION. The palate is the roof of
the mouth and floor of the nasal cavity. When it is not completely
formed, there is a cleft or longitudinal fissure between mouth and
nose. The lip and upper dental ridge may also be cleft, or only the
lip may be defective. In the latter case, early plastic surgery provides excellent repair so there is little defect of function or appearance. Until surgery is done, the sucking process may be poor.

Cleft palate surgery is needed for several reasons. The greatest
potential handicap because of palate insufficiency is a speech defect, which frequently includes missing teeth and improper alignment that needs surgical correction. Ear infections and impaired
hearing are also involved. Difficulty in eating, with choking and
possible aspiration, limitation of solid foods, and food entering
the nose are further distressing conditions than surgery should
correct. Surgery may be necessary more than once. The child in
school may not therefore have a complete correction of the defect.
Procedures that make eating comfortable can be done in the classroom or lunchroom of the school.

FEEDING TECHNIQUES FOR CLEFT PALATE. The use of thickened liquids avoids both choking and fluid entering nasal passage resulting from inability of the disordered oral mechanism to direct thin
liquids into the esophagus. Baby cereal, instant pudding, potato
flakes, or strained baby food can be used. Total iron intake should
be considered if prepared baby cereals are used, because they

contain an average of 7 milligrams of iron in ¼ cup, and the child over 3 years needs only 10 milligrams of iron daily. If an iron supplement is given daily, baby cereal would supply an excess.

Following lip repair, strained or mashed solid foods can be introduced at a normal age. Later, soft foods are placed between back teeth, with the child seated upright. The child must be aware of food placement and be able to manipulate it with good tongue control. If lateral tongue mobility is not present, pieces of food should not be introduced; only mashed or ground textures should be fed.

Development of oral function is an important component of therapy by the speech therapist. The feeding team may have to overcome fear and resistant behavior resulting from pain suffered following surgery, or oral defensiveness resulting from nasogastric tube feeding.

NUTRITIONAL CONCERNS WITH CLEFT PALATE. A common feeding pattern for the child with a cleft palate is prolonged feeding of bland foods, because acid irritates tender tissues. Since most foods rich in vitamin C are acidic, they are often omitted. A supplement of 40 mg/day vitamin C should be given to children from 3 to 10 years old, 45 milligrams for older children.

Intake of folic acid may also be inadequate. Green leafy vegetables, orange juice, organ meats, and egg yolk are rich in folacins. Since egg is the only one of these foods that is consumed by the child with a cleft palate, it is an important item in their diet. Unless there is a familial pattern of lipid (fat) disorders, egg can safely be fed daily. If there is no good food source of folic acid, a supplement should be given as prescribed by the health-care specialist. All other nutrients and calories can be supplied by a variety of wholesome foods that the child can eat.

Foods that should be avoided are spicy foods, nuts, popcorn, peanut butter, cooked cheese or creamed dishes, fruit peelings, and leafy vegetables.

HEREDITARY METABOLIC DISORDERS

Several hundred disorders have been reported as being the result of genetic mutations. Many hereditary metabolic disorders (HMD) have been identified and others hypothesized. They are characterized as inborn errors of the metabolism or transport of nutrients (Palmer and Ekvall, 1978). Most show evidence of clinical disease ranging from mild to fatal disorders.

Each genetic mutation in HMD affects specific enzymes. A specific enzyme may be altered so that it cannot function normally, or the quantity of enzyme may be inadequate, resulting in decrease or absence of function. Hereditary metabolic disorders can occur in the metabolism of all fuel nutrients, i.e., carbohydrate, protein, and lipids. They can also interfere with the body's use of vitamins in formation of coenzymes that are essential in the metabolic cycles.

When a HMD that is amenable to dietary treatment is diagnosed, the protocol is initiated with careful monitoring by the skilled team of a physician, nutritionist, nurse, social worker, and psychologist. A diet is planned to avoid amounts of the affected nutrient that will produce abnormal metabolites and will supply the normal metabolite that is not being produced (Crump, 1984). These disruptions of normal function can cause physical and mental damage leading to retardation and, in some disorders, if untreated, death. At this time, the only effective treatment is diet therapy (Acosta and Wenz, 1978).

PHENYLKETONURIA (PKU)

PKU is an inborn error of amino-acid metabolism that leads to mental retardation if it is not diagnosed and treated in early infancy.

Protein is composed of 22 amino acids, 8 of them essential for growth and life. Phenylalanine is an essential amino acid that is converted to tyrosine by the enzyme, phenylalanine hydroxylase. When the enzyme is absent, the amino acid is present in blood and urine in excessive amounts, along with its abnormal metabolites. This causes central nervous system and brain cells damage, which can be prevented by immediate dietary manipulation. Newborn screening for elevated blood levels of phenylalanine is mandatory in most of the United States. When PKU is found in a newborn infant, a formula is given in which the phenylalanine is decreased to provide only the amount necessary for good growth. Blood levels must be taken frequently to adapt the prescription to the individual infant. As the child grows, such foods as fruits, vegetables, fats, and some grain products low in phenylalanine are added to the diet. The nutritionist plans each diet change based on laboratory reports, anticipated growth and energy needs, with knowledge of the nutrient composition of all foods offered. Good dietary adherence typically results in normal physical and mental development.

The diet of persons with PKU is very restricted, and is often associated with management problems. For example, resistance to the formula or snitching of foods high in protein can lead to elevated blood phenylalanine levels. The child may not perceive the consequences of lack of compliance, but the parent may feel frustration and guilt, resulting in strained family relationships. One parent stated, "I feel more like a jailor than a mother." The clinic team members are often in close touch with the family and may be contacted by school staff for advice.

Children with PKU bring their food from home. Because of their restrictions, participation in school parties should be planned with their parents. The child can share punch or carbonated beverages, all fruits, and candy that does not contain chocolate or nuts. The child may bring his own low-protein treat to share with the class on special event. No emphasis should be placed on children with PKU as being different, but only that there are some foods they do not eat, like a child with an allergy to certain foods. They are normal in every other way, as was shown by Williamson, Koch, Azen, and Chang (1981). The Collaborative Study of Children Treated for Phenylketonuria concluded that involved persons should remain on the diet throughout life, whenever possible (Koch, Friedman, Williamson, and Azen, 1982). Therefore, acceptance of the child's dietary regimen by the school is very important to maintaining a healthy mind and self-image.

REFERENCES

Acosta, P.B., and Wenz, E. (1978). *Diet management of PKU: For infants and preschool children.* DHEW Publication No. HSA 78 –5209. Washington, DC: U.S. Government Printing Office.

Crump, I.M., (1984). Examples of metabolic errors. In D.G. Kelts and E.G. Jones (Eds.), *Manual of pediatric nutrition* (p. 209). Boston: Little, Brown.

Koch, R., Friedman, E., Williamson, M., and Azen, C. (1982). The collaborative study of diet discontinuation in phenylketonuric children, *Clinical Research.* 30(1), 118A.

Palmer, S., and Ekvall, S. (1978). Nutrition and hereditary metabolic disorders. In S. Palmer and S. Ekvall (Eds.), *Pediatric nutrition in developmental disorders*, p. 169. Springfield, Ill.: Charles C. Thomas.

Williamson, M.L., Koch, R. Azen, C., and Chang, C. (1981). Correlates of intelligence test results in treated phenylketonuric children. *Pediatrics 68*(2), 161.

CHAPTER 6

Conditions That Require
Special Dietary Management

Iris M. Crump

GASTROINTESTINAL DISORDERS

Gastroesophageal Reflux

This disorder is described as a backflow from the stomach that deposits gastric contents into the esophagus. It may be a benign developmental defect of the lower esophageal sphincter (valve) called the gastroesophageal junction. Acid juices cause a burning pain and vomiting. If sphincter incompetence continues, failure to thrive, esophageal stricture or ulceration, pulmonary aspiration, and pneumonia occur; bronchospasm and laryngospasm potentially result in asthma or apnea, (Richter and Castell, 1982). Diagnosis with an esophageal pH probe will determine extent and frequency of the backflow.

Dietary treatment of gastroesophageal reflux in the small child is by separating fluids and solid foods; e.g., a breakfast of toast and eggs is given at 7:00 a.m., but milk is withheld until 2½ to 3 hours later. This interval is repeated at each mealtime. Four small meals and four liquid feedings may be needed to avoid vomiting and achieve adequate weight gain. Antacids are given to the older child to neutralize the acid.

It has been thought that placing the child with poor head and trunk control in an infant seat or wheelchair decreases regurgitation of stomach contents into the esophagus. Several investigators, including Orenstein, Whitington, and Orenstein (1983), and Meyers and Herbst (1982), dispute this technique. They demonstrated that the infant or child who is prone had less reflex than when seated. X-rays showed the gastroesophageal junction submerged when the young child was seated. Additionally, when there is poor trunk control, the slumped position probably increases intra-abdominal pressure that would also predispose to reflux. It is often suggested that the head of the bed be elevated to reduce regurgitation.

Reflux appears to be reduced during sleep. The child stays awake when seated, perhaps preventing the benefit of relaxation during sleep. Since drowsiness commonly follows eating, it is an advantage to have the child lie down after lunch with the hope that sleep will occur and reduce reflux.

The hypotonic child may lack normal elasticity of the gastroesophageal sphincter. Closure can be weakened so that the stomach contents are not completely retained, resulting in frequent small regurgitations. Frequent small feedings reduce the acidity, and therefore reduce the chance of burning pain and damage to the esophagus.

Rumination and Vomiting

RUMINATION. Rumination is described as the voluntary or involuntary return of small amounts of food from the stomach to the mouth, to be either spit-out or rechewed and swallowed. It may be a symptom of over-eating, eating too fast, or swallowing air and belching, accompanied by food particles. It has no clinical significance, but is a distasteful process that can become a habit of the mentally retarded student. Most literature in the past described various pathological conditions related to rumination. Strawczynski (1964) reported on neuromuscular control of the gastroesophageal valve, which is the sphincter between esophagus and stomach. If there is a dysfunction of sympathetic and parasympathetic nervous systems, the sphincter may be continuously dilated, allowing upward passage of the stomach contents.

Nutritional status of the ruminator may be threatened if the process is continual and severe (Kalisz and Ekvall, 1978). Weight, height, and clinical signs of undernourishment, as well as supplementary data are needed to suggest status. Dentition may also be damaged.

More recently, psychological causes of rumination have been studied (Jackson, Johnson, Ackron, and Crowley, 1975). Maternal neglect of an infant, or inadequate attention in an institution, are examples of environments conducive to development of voluntary rumination.

Management of rumination requires team planning with the integral members of the school staff. Whether viewed as either a psychological problem (Hollowell and Gardner, 1965) or a physiological defect, a behavior management plan is essential. Rumination should be addressed vigorously when it first appears. If allowed to continue, the social stigmata of foul odor and stained clothing become greater than nutritional concerns.

Wright and Menolascino (1966) stressed forming a warm relationship and gradually involving the child in a group. The frequent pleasant interactions and calming environment seem effective. Ball, Hendricken, and Clayton (1974) demonstrated a feeding technique that emphasized tactile stimulation of the mouth rather than personal interaction. Both concepts could be incorporated into a health-care plan involving everyone who cares for the child.

VOMITING. Emesis, the propulsion of significant amounts of stomach contents out of the mouth is not simply a habit, but rather a symptom of another problem. Medical evaluation and recommendations are needed.

Constipation

Causes

Constipation is described as the infrequent passage of stools, or stools that are too dry or hard, resulting in incomplete evacuation of the colon. Most constipation seen in classes for handicapped children is not caused by abnormal bowel structure or disease. Usually it is the result of:

1. inadequate fiber and fluid in the diet
2. lessened awareness of the physical signal for defecation so that poor toileting habits have developed
3. drugs given for seizures, decreasing intestinal motility
4. spasticity or hypotonicity that slow the normal propulsive contractions of the colon
5. the child's fear of defecation because of pain or discomfort, resulting in resistance to having a bowel movement.

Physiological Processes

Digestion occurs mainly in the small intestine where the food is in a liquid form called chyme. The function of the large intestine is principally to allow fluid to be removed from the fecal mass to yield normal density on excretion. Fiber in foods holds fluid. It is not digested, but carries waste products and water out of the body. If the child is on strained or low-residue foods, there is no fiber. Most of the fluid in the chyme is then reabsorbed from the large intestine into the circulatory system. Decreased motility (peristalsis) caused by drugs or poor muscle tone results in increased transit time of the fecal mass. It takes longer to move through the large intestine, which is the ascending, transverse and descending colon. As a result, the dry stool is increasingly difficult for the weak abdominal muscles to propel out of the body.

Management

The treatment goal of constipation is to establish normal bowel habits that preclude pain or injury. Frequency is not as important as stool density.

1. *Medical management* is needed if the colon is impacted. When the colon is emptied, medication to maintain normal status may be required for several months while normal function and bowel habits are being restored (Kelts, 1984).

2. *Increase dietary fiber* for constipation. Bran is often suggested, but should not be given to a child without discussing it with the parents. They may be giving a maximum amount of bulking agent at home. Caution should be exercised in giving bran if the intestinal tract has been damaged; it may cause an irritable bowel with intermittent diarrhea and constipation. Caution is also needed to be sure that the material is being excreted: bowel movements at school should always be reported to parents, so that they do not assume regularity when it may not be happening.

3. *Natural vegetable powder (psillium seed).* Psillium seed is a cellulose that absorbs water, but is not digestible. One product is Metamucil®*, others are marketed with a drug company's label. Metamucil is useful for the child who has an irritable colon, as bran can further irritate

---

*G.D. Searle.

this condition, and children with esophageal problems cannot swallow bran. Natural vegetable powder is given in liquid or by spoon in pureed food followed by liquid. It is very important to drink the full amount of liquid recommended. The quantity of liquid that the powder absorbs is impressive and is the reason for its effectiveness in maintaining a soft (rubbery) stool. Caution is needed to be sure that the colon is emptied of hard material before any bulking agent is given. The school nurse can check for abdominal mass and keep a careful history of bowel movement.

4. *Food Sources of Fiber Are Important.* Strained and pureed food have little fiber value, but raw and cooked fruits and vegetables are valuable, even when mashed or chopped. Whole-grain products also contribute significant roughage, along with nuts and seeds. Meat, fish, eggs, milk, refined cereals, fats, and sugars are low in residue. Table 6–1 gives the total fiber content of a variety of foods.

5. *Liberal Fluid Intake Is Essential.* The average requirement is 1 ml/kcal intake of water (Czajka-Narino, 1984). For example, a child who consumes 1500 kilocalories needs 1500 milliliters of fluids, which is 50 ounces or 6 cups of water. Much of this water can come from food. Most fruits are high in fluid content, unless dried. Vegetables such as greens, summer squash, and cucumbers are excellent. The wide variation of water content in food is shown in Table 6–2.

   Fruits and vegetables are valuable for their fiber and nutrients, as well as their water content. Many can be put in a blender with some additional juice to make a tasty, thick beverage for the child who has difficulty swallowing (Figure 6–1).

   A dab of coconut syrup, a drop of vanilla, or a sprinkle of parmesan cheese will dress up a shake, and food coloring can make some appear more attractive. You can invent many more mixtures and will enjoy letting the child select items to make his or her own shake, watching the delight (or dismay) in drinking it!

   Fluids should be offered frequently between meals. Koolade and Gatorade contain dioctyl sodium succinate, a substance used as a stool softener, and, therefore, are useful in treating constipation.

6. *Regular Bowel Habits.* Promoted by school staff who toi-

Table 6–1. Average Dietary Fiber in Common Foods*

Vegetables		Breads and cereals		Fruit		Nuts	
Peas, raw	8	All Bran®	27	Pears (no skin)	2	Peanuts	9
Beans, baked	7	Puffed wheat®	15	Peaches (with skin)	2	Brazil nuts	8
Corn	5	Shredded wheat®	12	Strawberries	2		
Broccoli	4	Corn flakes	11	Apples (no skin)	1½		
Carrots	3½	Whole meal bread	8½	Bananas	1¾		
Potatoes	3½	Special K®	5	Grapefruit, canned	½		
Lettuce	1½	White bread	3	Mandarin oranges	¼		

There are several classes of dietary fiber that vary in retrieval depending on the technique of extraction. This table gives averages from several sources for a general concept of relative content of total fiber in food.
*Grams per 100 grams edible portion.

let their students regularly, especially after meals. Training is a valid objective in the child's health care program.

Megacolon

Massive, abnormal dilation of the colon with fecal material describes megacolon. Cause may be congenital, toxic or acquired.

Toxic megacolon is the result of ulcerative colitis, and medical intervention is urgent.

Hirschsprung's disease is a congenital disorder in which the

Table 6–2. Percentages of Water in Some Foods*

Lettuce	96%	Watermelon	93%
Green beans	94	Canned pears	91
Carrots	91	Orange	88
Potato	80	Banana	76
Cooked cereal	87	Milk	87
Bread	40	Egg	74
Crackers	4	Lean beef	60

*Nutritive Value of Foods (1964) *Home and garden bulletin* (No. 72). Washington, D.C.: U.S. Dept. of Agriculture.

Apple and celery with pineapple juice

Cooked prunes with syrup and pear

Cooked carrots and raisins with their juice

Celery with tomato juice

Cucumber (no seeds) with grapefruit

Zucchini (small) with tomato juice

Watermelon (no liquid needed)

Orange with peaches

Figure 6–1. Some appetizing beverages for children who have trouble swallowing.

smooth-muscle wall of the colon lacks autonomic ganglia, causing massive dilation. Diagnosed by biopsy, surgery is necessary. The affected area is removed; colostomy may be needed while the resected bowel heals.

Acquired megacolon is the result of inability or refusal to defecate, with dilation by impacted feces. Abdominal pain and overflow diarrhea (encopresis) can sometimes be misleading until an abdominal examination reveals the problem. Medical management is needed, with careful introduction and gradual increase of food bulk. The school nurse may be asked to participate in giving medications and reporting results to physician and parents.

Constipation is often overlooked by physicians, but is of grave concern to parents and teachers who see discomfort, pain when stooling, and loss of appetite in the handicapped child.

Diarrhea

Diarrhea is increased frequency or volume of stool, or both. The consistency is liquid, and loss of 20 mg/kg/day or greater is considered serious. Acute diarrhea lasts a few days; chronic diarrhea usually persists for 3 weeks or longer.

Clinical Description

A thorough history of diarrhea should include all food and fluid intake, vomiting (if present), and stools that include frequency, quantity, and appearance. School staff will be asked to participate in collection of this data, and the school nurse will relate information to the child's physician. Weights and clinical signs are important: loss of 10 percent body weight is critical, and poor skin turgor, sunken eyes, circles under eyes, and listlessness are significant signs of dehydration, as well as dry, cracked lips and decreased urination. They should be reported to the nurse.

Physiological Process

Impaired intestinal absorption of all major nutrients, including water, occurs with acute diarrhea, resulting in dehydration and malnutrition if the process is not corrected. The mucosal and absorptive surface of the intestinal tract is damaged and function impaired. Secretion of enzymes necessary for lactose (milk sugar) and other disaccharides (sugars) to be digested may be decreased or absent. The presence of these unabsorbed sugars leads to bacterial overgrowth amd increased fermentation in the intestinal tract. The organic acids formed cause fluid to be drawn into the gut with resultant liquid stool—fluid loss that leads to dehydration. The sugar source may be a clear liquid, which is often prescribed when a child has diarrhea. Carbonated beverages, fruit juices, and fruit-flavored drinks are high in sucrose or fructose. These liquids contribute to diarrhea in a second manner because they are high in osmolality that also draws fluid into the intestinal tract. In this way, diarrhea is continued rather than relieved.

Nutritional Therapy

ACUTE DIARRHEA. The primary objective in therapy for acute diarrhea is the replacement of fluid and caloric losses while providing for current nutritional needs.

1. Usually clear liquids are prescribed for the first 24 to 48 hours. Fruit juices, fruit-flavored drinks, such as Koolade or Hi-C, should not be given at this time. For the small child, Pedialyte®*, Lytren®† or one of the other commercially prepared electrolyte solutions are prescribed. For the older child, Gatorade, weak tea, or diluted Hawaiian Punch can be used.
2. Solid foods should be introduced gradually.
3. Milk should be tried cautiously. If diarrhea resumes, a beverage containing no lactose should be substituted for 2 to 3 weeks. The child may not like soy-based formulas. A cultured yogurt may be well-tolerated because the culture organisms can change lactose in milk to a carbohydrate that is tolerated.

CHRONIC DIARRHEA. Diarrhea lasting more than 3 weeks and unresponsive to the dietary management described above is often caused by injury to the intestine after an infection. There are several causes, most of which can be ruled out or identified by laboratory analysis or biopsy. Diagnosis must be established before nutritional therapy can be prescribed.

A condition that is frustrating to everyone is irritable bowel syndrome. The pediatrician sees a child with episodes of diarrhea interspersed with normal or hard stools, not diagnosed or responsive to treatment, yet the child is otherwise healthy and growing well. The mother sees her child as responding with diarrhea to every minor illness or emotional upset. The teacher sees the discouraging recurrence of diarrhea that necessitates the child's missing school. The school nurse sees a frequently soiled, smelly child who is a worry because he may be spreading an infection or parasite throughout the school.

When diagnostic studies and usual dietary treatment are unsuccessful in solving the problem, careful family, stool, and dietary histories may indicate irritable bowel syndrome. This condition is characterized by chronic, nonspecific diarrhea in an otherwise healthy child who is growing normally. In this instance the usual low-fat, clear-liquid diet that is often prescribed, may exacerbate the symptoms. Therefore, introduction of a regular diet is needed, starting with starches, then meats, fruits and veg-

---

*Ross Laboratories
†Mead Johnson

etables, and lastly, milk products. The disorder usually diminishes by 3½ to 4 years of age. It may continue longer, but still can only be treated in the same way, with attention to the illness or upset that triggered it. Understanding and cooperation among all persons involved will reduce the threat of mistrust and misunderstanding; remember that the child also is unhappy with the situation.

INFECTIOUS DISEASES

The sequelae of infectious diseases frequently involve many body systems, and can be permanent or rehabilitative. Some of the infections that commonly result in conditions needing special dietary considerations are described in this section.

Sequelae of Transplacental Infections

The outcome of infections occuring during pregnancy can be fetal mortality or congenital malformations involving compromised motor, mental, gastrointestinal, and pulmonary functions. Examples are rubella and cytomegalic virus. Etiology of the disorder may not be verifiable, but suspected because of the type of damage observed. Careful monitoring of the treatment usually involves many school specialists. Diet therapy may be specific, prescribed by the physician or health care provider, and planned by the dietitian. In other instances, feeding may be planned with input from the school nurse and occupational or speech therapist.

Often the child is being treated for failure to thrive. Special formula and frequent feedings may be required at school as well as at home.

Sequelae of Central Nervous System Infections

Encephalitis is an inflamatory condition of the brain usually caused by the bite of an infected mosquito; it may also be the result of poisoning or hemorrhage. Early diagnosis and supportive treatments have reduced deaths and serious disability resulting from encephalitis. When seizures occur, however, the child will need medication that can interfere with nutrient utilization (see Chapter 2, Drug-Nutrient Interactions). Another outcome may be severe spasticity for which the child will require special equipment and a soft diet. Chapter 4 gives guidelines for this intervention.

Meningitis is an infection or inflamation of the membranes covering the brain and spinal cord. It is caused by bacteria, virus, chemical irritation, or tumor. Antibiotics have decreased the mortality resulting from meningitis. However, serious sequelae are severe retardation, seizures, spasticity, strabismus, and poor motor coordination. Soft diet, a special wheelchair, and extended meal periods are often needed (see the section, Menu Adaptations for the Soft Diet in Chapter 8).

Food-Borne Bacterial Infections

Exposure to various agents causing infections, from the common cold to pneumonia, is increased in the schoolroom. Consistent caution by the staff, with handwashing between feeding each child, and not sharing towels between students will decrease exposure. A major cause of influenza is food contaminated by bacteria or their toxins. It is difficult to keep food covered and hot food *hot* or cold food *cold*. A food thermometer should be used to insure that no food sits in the classroom or kitchen at temperatures between 40° and 110°F Farenheit beyond the meal period. If there is a delay in serving a hot food, it should be refrigerated, then reheated when served. Cooked food held overnight in the refrigerator should be heated to 212°F for 3 minutes. Precautions are necessary because of increased exposure to contamination during transportation as well as increased handling of foods in schoolrooms, as is often done in special education classes, compared to rigid cafeteria regulations. Students in these classrooms are often more medically fragile than nonhandicapped school children and, consequently, are more susceptible to infections.

Gastroenteritis

Food poisoning, dysentery, and typhoid fever are infections that cause gastroenteritis. In each, vomiting and diarrhea result in dehydration and loss of substances necessary to maintain body equilibrium.

Diagnosis is essential so that appropriate treatment can be initiated. When several children in the same school become ill at the same time, they may have eaten contaminated food. Samples of food served can be examined for pathogens, or preparation and handling of the food traced. Food handlers should be checked to detect Staphylococcus carriers if the gastritis reoccurs frequently.

Hospitalization for parenteral feeding may be necessary when fever and vomiting are prolonged. Food is usually withheld, and liquids increased as tolerated. The section, Diarrhea, gives appropriate recommendations once etiology is established.

MALNUTRITION

Malnutrition is described as the condition of poor growth and illness resulting from an insufficient amount or imbalance of nutrients, or inadequate utilization of food intake. Severe calorie and protein malnutrition is called marasmus, and results in progressive wasting of the entire body. Kwashiorkor is the result of severe protein deficiency: distended belly and thin extremities with pitting edema are typical characteristics. If either condition occurs in early childhood, deficits in intellectual ability may occur.

Deficiencies of individual nutrients were discussed in Chapter 1. Many studies have been done to corroborate interpretation of deficiencies in children. Pollitt, Saco-Pollitt, Leibel, and Viteri (1986) reviewed the main findings of effects of iron deficiency on cognitive function among infants and preschool children. They summarized:

> In populations where there is a high prevalance of protein–energy malnutrition, iron deficient infants and preschool children tend to be smaller and lighter than children without signs of iron deficiency; in these populations, the iron-deficient infants and preschool children are not likely to improve their performance in mental developmental scales and specific measures of cognitive function following iron repletion therapy (pp. 555-565).

Protein-calorie malnutrition and related iron deficiency occur in infants and young children who have defects that limit proper food intake. Many organs and systems may be damaged, including poor absorptive surface of the intestinal tract and inadequate synthesis of digestive enzymes. As a result, the nutrients in food ingested are not well utilized. Therefore, more food needs to be eaten, or products that are easier to digest need to be given. Table 6-3 offers ways to increase calories and protein in daily meals. Nutritional supplements should be prescribed by a nutrition consultant who is a registered dietition (RD), or by a health-care provider who knows the child.

In addition to the increase in nutrient need due to poor intestinal integrity, respiratory stress with cardiac damage and muscle spasticity expend more energy than normal structures (Eddy, Nicholson, and Wheeler, 1965). Supplying extra carbohydrate and

Table 6–3. More Per Bite*

EACH ITEM WILL INCREASE CALORIES BY 120:	
At Mealtimes	
1 tbsp oil, butter, or margarine	Twice the calories of an equal amount of protein or carbohydrate. One tsp added per meal will not appreciably change the taste, texture, or quantity of food.
Between Meals	
cup grape juice ¾ cup jello ½ cup sherbet	These foods contain no fat and supply needed fluid as well as calories. Fats decrease stomach emptying time. They should not be fed between meals to a child whose appetite is poor.
Evening	
½ cup ice cream 2 rounded tbsp grated or cream cheese 1 rounded tbsp peanut butter	Served in the evening as a fourth meal, these high fat foods will have emptied from the stomach by morning.
EACH ITEM WILL INCREASE PROTEIN BY 7 GRAMS	
⅓ cup dry non-fat milk	Add several tbsp to cooked cereal, soup, pudding, mashed potatoes, or fluid milk.
1 large egg (poached lightly) ½ jar junior meat 1 oz. cheese ¼ cup cottage cheese	Add to casseroles, vegetables, soup, scrambled eggs.

*Foods that are high in calories and protein can be added to meals to provide "more per bite" without significantly affecting taste, texture, or volume.

fat for calories also increases the need for more of the specific vitamins needed for their metabolism. Vitamins and minerals can be supplied in concentrated supplements, but energy (calories) and protein must be supplied by food.

If calories from fat and carbohydrate are inadequate for energy needs, protein is used for energy before it is available for building tissue.

General health is also vulnerable to protein/calorie malnutrition. Resistance to infection is the task of leucocytes, which are white blood cells that require protein, iron, and the vitamins that participate in their metabolism. Among the most important functions of leucocytes are to (1) digest bacteria and viruses; (2) detoxify proteins resulting from allergic reactions; and (3) develop immunities. The frequent illnesses of handicapped students may be the result of inadequate intake or utilization of the nutrients needed to produce leucocytes.

Obesity resulting from excessive calorie intake is also a form of malnutrition. Causes and a control regimen are in Chapter 7. Many factors that can cause an unbalanced, insufficient or excessive food intake in the school can contribute to malnutrition. Causes of malnutrition in school-aged children include the following:

1. Lack of nutrition education can result in poor food choices.
2. Lack of communication skill limits what the child can express about his or her feelings of pain, hunger, or thirst. Rejection of food may be because it is too hot or salty, or the student dislikes the taste rather than because the student is not hungry.
3. Poor motor coordination can make feeding so difficult that a limited mealtime or fatigue does not allow the child to get enough food each meal.
4. Spillage is often disregarded; more food may end up on the outside rather than inside the child.
5. Energy (calorie) and nutrient needs may be increased because of malabsorption or increased expenditure due to cardiac malfunction, athetosis, infection, or other stress.
6. Absence of appetite can be caused by central nervous system disorder.
7. Bizarre eating habits can result from indulgence by family members who feel that giving their child freedom in food choices compensates for limitations in other abilities.
8. Hyperactivity increases a child's energy expenditure and decreases his attention span so that mealtime is interrupted frequently.
9. School lunches may not provide foods the child can eat.

Teachers and their staff deal with these and other problems daily. Meals are a small but essential part of the school day's program.

NUTRITIONAL MANAGEMENT OF
MALNUTRITION IN CHILDREN

1. Use foods of highest nutrient content. In general, the more a food is processed the more nutrients are lost. Therefore, prepared baby food and pureed items are less desirable than table foods. For example, in a meat portion, 100 g of strained beef has 13.4 g protein and 94 kcal; 100 g of simmered beef has 27 g protein and 288 kcal.

2. Increase caloric content of food. Carbohydrate and protein each contribute 4 kcal/g. Fat contributes 9 kcal/g. One teaspoon of margarine, butter, or oil contains 40 kcal and does not appreciably change the volume, taste, or texture of the food to which it is added. The food service center can be asked to send a cube of margarine or butter, or a bottle of salad oil as needed for a class of children if some need extra calories. One tablespoon of either kind of fat can be added daily to the foods of underweight children who are not on a prescribed diet.

3. Use special equipment to adapt regular foods sent for the school meals. A food grinder or blender should be provided for the classrooms having children who cannot eat the foods sent because of limitations in chewing. All items not amenable to change in texture should be replaced with foods of comparable nutrient value by the food service department.

4. Foods that must be softened should have the added moisture from nutrient-rich liquids, such as concentrated cream soups, milk, or fruit juices instead of water.

5. Give more frequent, smaller feedings with low-fat foods between meals, and high fat foods at mealtimes. Fat decreases stomach emptying. Snacks should therefore be high carbohydrate, which will not remain in the stomach long enough to decrease appetite for the next meal.

ALLERGY

Definition of Allergy

The term is misused as representing undefined responses, such as hyperactivity, by some procedures that do not provide acceptable evidence of an immunological reaction (May, 1979). In this section only allergy to food is discussed.

Manifestation and Diagnosis of Allergy

Food is easily blamed for many gastrointestinal, respiratory, and skin conditions. Progressive exclusion of foods suspected of causing allergies may increase until the child is malnourished and unnecessarily limited.

Symptoms described as food allergy must be thoroughly evaluated by a physician. Teachers and school nurses contribute valuable observation in a more objective setting than the home. After discussion with the family and physician, the help of a dietitian is needed to set up a carefully controlled study of the condition followed by a regimen agreed to by everyone involved in the child's care.

The physician will want history and clinical evidence of manifestations including:

1. gastrointestinal disturbances, such as frequent diarrhea, abdominal pain, or vomiting
2. skin rash or eczema
3. respiratory problems of wheezing, chronic coughing, ear, and sinus infections

The symptoms described could stem from bacteria or parasitic infections, enzyme disorders, chemical contamination, or emotional distress, as well as from food allergy. The physician will ask for school staff's help in defining the occurrence of symptoms. Verification is by agreement of all diagnostic procedures including *valid* tests and food changes if appropriate. Most frequently used procedures are described briefly below.

AN ELIMINATION DIET. This may be prescribed in which wheat, milk, eggs, and other common sensitizers are omitted. It cannot be used for young children for over a month without resulting in nutritional deficiencies. Foods are added individually in 2-week intervals so that intermediate and long-range, as well as immediate, hypersensitivities can be exposed. The food is omitted if symptoms precipitating the search recur. It should be introduced again at a later time to confirm the reaction; it should not be assumed to be the offender after only one or even two trials. All items that contain the food being tested must be eliminated.

The nutritionist or dietitian will provide specific instructions so that the challenge or elimination diet is not faulted by unintentional inclusion of a food, beverage, or medication containing the factor being assessed. All school staff who work with the child should be alerted. They will be asked to keep careful records of all oral intake, including the source of water.

SKIN TESTING. Skin testing is appropriate only in children over 3 years of age and for immediate-type allergic reactions, as explained by May (1979). It is not considered highly conclusive because a wheal may appear even when food is tolerated. After unnecessary discomfort from the antigen in the scratch- or intradermal test, restrictions that are not necessary can be the result.

REINTRODUCTION OF THE SUSPECTED FOOD after all symptoms have cleared is a challenge (Adams and Mahan, 1984). The optimal form of challenge is a double blind in which neither child nor parent knows what is in the capsule prepared for the test. In a single blind challenge, only the child is unaware of being challenged. The test food may have to be disguised in another food if the child cannot swallow a capsule. In an open challenge, the child also knows he is eating the suspected antigen. Caution must be exercised to avoid alerting the child to expect symptoms.

"ENVIRONMENTAL AGENTS." These are blamed for allergies by a group called clinical ecologists. A rotation diet is used to determine allergic reactions: the patient decides which food groups are "safe." The decision often is highly subjective and verification unclear (Williams, 1985). Further discussion of this concept will follow under Management of Food Allergy.

INTESTINAL BIOPSY AND LABORATORY STUDIES OF IMMUNE RESPONSES. Used in selected cases, they are not appropriate for all suspected allergies.

Management of Food Allergy

Eliminating all forms of an offending food requires careful planning. For example, a reaction to milk allergy could occur after eating milk chocolate, bread, or margarine containing milk, sherbet, or many other prepared foods that may contain small amounts of milk. Some children tolerate those small amounts; controlled intake is then allowed. The nutritionist will prescribe the diet, along with the allergist. They will ask for the school's food service director to let the teacher know which foods in the monthly menu contain the offending food. The school should not be expected to provide a special diet; it should be sent from home. When possible, part of the school lunch should be offered to the allergic child so that he does not feel "different" or excluded from the important social experience of mealtime.

Excluding foods to which a child is allergic may produce nutritional deficiencies, if no replacement is provided. For example, milk supplies most calcium and riboflavin, both essential nutrients. A supplement can be given; flavored wafers containing calcium and a vitamin-B complex chewable tablet are the most effective replacements when it is almost impossible to get enough from other foods.

Many food intolerances tend to be resolved as the child grows older (Bock, 1982). Allergies diagnosed in the child under 3 years of age are not as likely to lessen with age than those defined later. It is important to rechallenge in 6 to 12 months so that foods are not unnecessarily restricted.

A common misunderstanding is the assumption that a child is allergic to milk when the physician recommends a soy product and excludes milk when a child has repeated or chronic episodes of diarrhea. The doctor's concern is that secretion of the enzyme lactase is decreased or absent so that the sugar in milk (lactose) is not metabolized. The result is perpetration of the diarrhea. Soy products contain no lactose, so the problem is avoided. However, the child will recover and probably not return to the physician, but parents will feel that milk is permanently eliminated. Instead, damage to the intestinal tract usually heals in a few weeks so that lactase levels are restored. Milk should be introduced gradually to induce further secretion of lactase. Full tolerance usually is achieved.

Some medications may be prescribed, but are supportive rather than solutions to food allergies.

REFERENCES

Adams, E.J., Mahan, L.K. (1984). Nutritional care in food allergy and food intolerance. *Food, Nutrition and Diet Therapy* (pp. 633-653). Philadelphia: W.B. Saunders.

Ball, T.S., Hendricksen, H., and Clayton, J. (1974). A special feeding technique for chronic regurgitation. *American Journal on Mental Deficiency 78,* 486.

Bock, S.A. (1982). The natural history of food sensitivity. *Allergy and Clinical Immunology 69*, 173.

Czajka-Narino, D.M. (1984). Water and electrolytes. In M.V. Krause and L.K. Mahan (Eds.), *Food, nutrition and diet therapy* (p. 183). Philadelphia: W.B. Saunders.

Eddy, T.P., Nicholson, A.L., and Wheeler, E.F. (1965). Energy expenditures and dietary intakes in cerebral palsy. *Developmental Medicine and Child Neurology 7*, 377.

Greene, H., and Schubert, W. (1979). Diarrhea and malabsorption. In (Ed.), *Pediatric nutrition handbook* (p. 190). American Academy of Pediatrics.

Hollowell, J.G. and Gardner, L.I. (1965). Rumination and growth failure in male fraternal twin-associated with disturbed family environment. *Pediatrics 36*, 565.

Jackson, G.M., Johnson, C.R., Ackron, G.S., and Crowley, R. (1975). Food satiation as a procedure to decelerate vomiting. *American Journal of Mental Deficiency, 80*(2), 223-227.

Kalisz, K., and Ekvall, S. (1978). Rumination. In S. Palmer and Ekvall (Eds.), *Pediatric Nutrition in Developmental Disorders* (p. 165). Springfield, Ill.: Charles C. Thomas.

Kelts, D.G. (1984). Principal problems of the digestive system. In D.G. Kelts and E.G. Jones (Eds.), *Manual of Pediatric Nutrition* (p. 167). Boston: Little, Brown.

May, C.D. (1979). Diagnosis of hypersensitivity to food, *Pediatric Nutrition Handbook* (pp. 355-365). Evanston, Ill.: American Academy of Pediatrics.

Meyers, W.F., Herbst J.J. (1982). Effectiveness of positioning therapy for gastroesophageal reflux. *Pediatrics 69*, 768-72.

Nutritive Value of Foods, (1964). *Home and garden bulletin* No. 72. Appendix table 1. Washington, DC: U.S. Department of Agriculture.

Orenstein, S.R., Whitington, P.F., and Orenstein, D.M. (1983).

The infant seat as treatment for gastroesophageal reflux. *New England Journal of Medicine 309* (19),760-763.

Pollitt, E., Saco-Pollitt, C., Leibel, R.L., and Viteri, F.E. (1986). Iron deficiency and behavioral development in infants and pre-school chldren. *American Journal of Clinical Nutrition, 43*(4), 555-565.

Richter, J.E., and Castell, D.O. (1982). Gastroesophageal reflux pathogenesis, diagnosis and therapy. *American Internal Medicine 97*, 93-103.

Strawczynski, H. (1964). The behavior of the lower esophageal sphincter in infants and its relationship to gastroesophageal regurgitation. *Journal of Pediatrics 64*, 17.

Williams, S.W. (1985). *Nutrition and diet therapy* (p. 809). St. Louis: Times Mirror/Mosby.

Wright, M.M., and Menolascino, F.J. (1966). Nuturant nursing of mentally retarded ruminators. *American Journal on Mental Deficiency, 9*, 451.

CHAPTER 7

Group Program for Weight Control

Iris M. Crump

FACTORS CONTRIBUTING TO OVERWEIGHT

Obesity is defined as body weight in excess of that needed for body function. In this chapter, a person who is at least 20 percent above desirable weight will be considered obese. The Society of Actuaries and Life Insurance Medical Directors of America (1980) released standards which contradicted previous weight tables distributed by Metropolitan Life Insurance Company. The new figures suggest a higher weight ratio for both women and men. The recommended range for men's weight was increased by 15 to 20 pounds, as related to age and height. Standards for women's weight increased also. For example, the 1980 recommended weight range for women 4 feet, 11 inches to 5 feet, 2 inches in height was 10 pounds higher than the previous weight range, because epidemiological studies of the American population's health did not indicate that improved health status resulted from the lower weight. Obesity is a major health hazard in the United States and other affluent countries. Prevalence among adults is estimated to be between 15 and 50 percent. Although innumerable programs are offered for weight control, there is a high attrition rate during programs, with limited weight loss, and poor maintenance of any weight lost following completion of a program (Brownell and Stunkard, 1980). Countless books and articles have been published on the subject, yet most obese adults claim they have unsuccessfully "tried everything" in their attempts to lose excess pounds.

It is obvious that prevention of obesity and intervention early in life is the viable alternative to attempts to change adult life styles related to eating.

Young children learn change more rapidly and accept appropriate behaviors more readily than older persons (Rozin, 1980). It therefore becomes a high priority to address the problem during school years.

Genetic Versus Environmental Causes of Overweight

A critical factor that contributes to overwieght is the family environment. Many studies have been done comparing body-fat measurements of parents and children. Khoury (1983) compared parents and their children under 20 years of age, who resided in the parents' home, with parents and adult offspring who did not live at home. Significant correlations of body fat measurements of parents and children living at home were shown, but no similarity in fatness was found between parents and offspring out of the home.

A large epidemiological study of obesity was done by Hartz, Gieter, and Rimm (1977). The effects of parental example and child-rearing techniques were compared to heredity for 26,100 children aged 4 to 11 years. Family environment was shown to be responsible for 32 to 39 percent of the variation in obesity. Genetic factors contributing to obesity were present in only 11 percent of the children.

Some investigators (Borjeson, 1980, Brinker, 1981) suggest that body type may be inherited, with the environment then contributing to normal or excessive weight gain.

Control of Eating Behavior by the Child as a Cause of Overweight

The handicapped child may learn to manipulate parents or caretakers by refusing some foods and demanding what he or she likes. This relationship may be well established before the child enters school.

The Impact of Food Restrictions on Social Interactions

Everyone who is responsible for restricting food must consider the implications for disruption of relationships between the person restricted and peers, family, and other persons with whom interaction occurs. Food preferences, eating habits, and mealtime rituals are disturbed as well. Giving food is a primary aspect of motherliness; strong bonding is developed by a mother's satisfying her infant's hunger. Both are rewarded when the baby is fed; mother has the assurance of nourishing her baby and the infant develops trust by having the hunger satiated. Therefore, changing the relationship of mother giving the child what he or she wants to eat disrupts their concepts of each other. Parents of handicapped children in particular are often hesitant or unwilling to relinquish the strong bond that giving food has established between them and their child. They may understand that overweight creates problems, but do not express their reluctance because they feel it is one of the few enjoyments they share when handicaps limit the child's participation in other activities. *Therefore, the first change to be made in planning a weight control regimen is to find an alternative activity for parent and child to share instead of allowing unlimited eating.*

The process of change is effective when the intervention is transdisciplinary and involves school staff, parents, physician, and nutrition consultant. Agreement on a plan needs support from all persons involved. Once parents are comfortable with a compensatory interaction with their child, assessment, goals, and a weight-control plan are designed.

A GROUP WEIGHT-CONTROL PROGRAM

A group program is more successful than individual effort to lose weight, because of the powerful influence of peer support.

The outline of a group weight-control program and instruction for its use will follow in Appendixes 7–1 and 7–2. In Chapter 9 a complete curricula will be developed for some sessions of the program. The program has been used successfully in San Diego County, California, for more than 10 years. Initially, a nutrition consultant conducted sessions at the San Diego Regional Center for the Developmentally Disabled. When it was demonstrated that goals (Appendix 7–1) could be accomplished, the weight-management program was discussed with the educational consultant, who then prepared it to be offered to school, workshops, and rehabilitation centers for handicapped students throughout the county. A meeting was held with principals and directors of facilities indicating an interest. Plans were made for the program to be integrated into their curriculum. Staff members were appointed to coordinate and conduct the program. A workshop was held to train persons involved. The training was conducted by the nutrition consultant, psychologist and occupational therapist. Ways to implement change in food intake, eating behavior, and exercise activities were discussed. Experience demonstrated that facilities using only parts of the program had poor success in achieving weight loss; all three components must be implemented with the participation of families.

Benefits of Facility-Conducted Weight Management Programs

The benefits of having facilities conduct their own programs were evident:

1. From the principal to the security officer, all staff were enthusiastic and eager for success; there are not many such measureable, visible accomplishments for persons who are multiply handicapped.
2. The participants and their parents were proud of accomplishing weight control; they had worked together to achieve it (parents, also, frequently lost weight by following program guidelines).
3. Participants felt part of a group by helping and being helped to stay on the diet. Improvement was impressive in the participants' self-esteem, decision making, motivation and self control.
4. Parents gained insight from other parents having similar problems; they did not feel alone and defeated in trying to control their child's weight.
5. Improved rapport was established between school staff and parents by weekly contacts concerning the students' progress in the program.

ASSESSMENT OF THE OVERWEIGHT CHILD

1. *Physical examination of the child*, including visual observation is an important factor in determining overweight in the child in special education classes. Physical handicaps change the growth process and distribution of both lean and fat body-mass. For example, the nonambulatory child may develop extensive truncal obesity, but have principally lean muscle mass in arms and

shoulders. Tables of normal skinfold measurements would not be appropriate indicators of that child's status. Again, the 18-year-old student having Down syndrome may be the height shown on growth graphs for the average 12-year-old child; organ mass is age-appropriate, however, so that weight for height would be expected to be higher in the 18-year-old than the graph would indicate.

2. *Diet history and records of current food intake* provide critical information about the reason for excessive weight. The dietitian or nutritionist can assess calorie and nutrient intake, as well as further information about family meal patterns.

3. *Health and growth records and history of food intake* can be collected by the school nurse or health care provider. A record of physical activity at school and home is also needed.

4. *Attitudes toward food,* including appetite, food preferences, and such eating behaviors as rapid eating, stealing or begging for food, and excessive drinking (even of water) can be observed by all school personnel who work with the student.

5. *Essential information about parental attitudes and control* in the home, as well as family eating habits can be provided by a parent conference with school staff.

A case conference is usually scheduled to summarize all information. It is valuable to have the psychologist or counselor, included with key staff, parents, and the nutrition consultant. An individual education program (IEP) could incorporate a weight-management program into the student's school schedule along with a plan to assist the family in supporting the goal of weight control.

The following regimen for weight management is a thoroughly tested program that has proven to be successful in 17 educational centers for handicapped persons. A nutrition consultant is essential for the training of course instructors, setting of appropriate weight goals, instruction of parents in dietary control, coordinating other specialists, scheduling individual counseling as needed, and assuring that credit is given to the assiduous staff persons who conduct the sessions. An explanation of conducting the regimen follows in Appendix 7–1.

CONDUCTING THE WEIGHT-CONTROL PROGRAM

The program design was developed by the author and Marydale Dessel, M.S., R.D., with consultation provided by an education consultant, psychologist, occupational therapist, and school nurse. A letter describing the program may be sent to all schools and workshops for handicapped and developmentally delayed children and adolescents. The best response may be generated by addressing the letter to the principal or program director with a copy to the nursing or therapy unit. A workshop to clarify all components of a succesful program is essential; facilities that modified the curriculum were disappointed with poor outcome.

Potential participants are selected by the teacher and nurse, and a letter is sent to each family, stressing the many positive aspects of this program, and reassuring them that adverse attention or attitude will not occur. They are invited to attend the first group session for more information. Participation of the family unit is also essential; for participants who are living independently, the roommate or other concerned person should attend the three sessions to provide much-needed support.

Contracts for parents and participants add committment to follow-through (Figures 7–1 and 7–2); it is not presented as a threat, but rather to emphasize the importance of their role in the program's success.

Individual folders are assembled; participants design their own covers. The folders contain a copy of their contract (Figure 7–2); attendance record (Figure 7–3); weekly weight report (Figure 7–4); the "Watch My Weight Go Down" chart (Figure 7-5); food record (Figure 7–6); home assignment (Figure 7–7); activities done in class and at home; hand-outs; Select-A-Meal®*; exercises pictured as stick figures; and a membership badge.

The group members choose their group name and make their membership badge. One group chose the name HELP to represent "Help Each other Lose Pounds." Some guidance is needed, but each member will feel proud of their unique identity.

Select-A-Meal* is a colorful booklet of the seven food groups with pictures of some foods in portion size, pictures of cups or spoons next to other foods to indicate a serving, and special measurements for meats. A personal meal plan pictures each food group with space for the daily number of servings of each. The Select-A-Meal is used to instruct both participants and parents; it is used throughout the program by giving meal planning variety within a structured plan. Food models, both plastic simulations and paper pictures, make the program appropriate for moderately retarded participants who are unable to read and write.

Some facilities use a 1200-calorie diet for all participants. Others modify individual plans according to the weight goal and

---

*American Diabetes Association, North Carolina Affiliate, Inc. Station Square, Suite 50, Rocky Mount, NC 27801

Figure 7-1. Example of weight control program contract for parents or caretakers.

WEIGHT CONTROL PROGRAM CONTRACT FOR PARENTS

Name of Participant _____

Parent Name _____

Telephone Number _____

Address _____

I (name)_____ will
participate in 3 parent meetings of the weight control program. I will provide
the diet which I will help to plan for _____ .

From *Nutrition and Feeding of the Handicapped Child,* by Iris M. Crump. © 1987 by College-Hill Press, a division of Little, Brown, and Company, Inc. Reproduction of this material for any purpose other than clinical work or training is prohibited.

Figure 7-2. Example of weight control contract for participants in the program.

WEIGHT CONTROL PROGRAM CONTRACT FOR PARTICIPANTS

Name of Participant _____

Parent Name _____

Telephone Number _____

Address _____

I, (name)_____ will
participate in group meetings of the weight control program. I will plan and
follow the diet that will help me lose weight.

From *Nutrition and Feeding of the Handicapped Child,* by Iris M. Crump. © 1987 by College-Hill Press, a division of Little, Brown, and Company, Inc. Reproduction of this material for any purpose other than clinical work or training is prohibited.

Figure 7-3. Example of an attendance record for participants in the weight control program.

ATTENDANCE RECORD							
Program Name _____ Location _____							
Name of Participants	DATES ATTENDED						
Name of Parents	DATES ATTENDED						

Figure 7-4. Example of weight control program weight chart.

WEIGHT CONTROL PROGRAM

Program name: _____

Location: _____ Coordinator: _____

Name of Participant	DATE	Weekly Weight									

Figure 7-5. "Watch My Weight Go Down!" chart for weight control program.

WATCH MY WEIGHT GO DOWN!

Starting Weight: _____   Name _____

Goal Weight: _____   Birth Date: _____

← Weeks →

Pounds	1	2	3	4	5	6	7	8	9	10	11	12	How did I do?

← Dates →

From *Nutrition and Feeding of the Handicapped Child,* by Iris M. Crump. © 1987 by College-Hill Press, a division of Little, Brown, and Company, Inc. Reproduction of this material for any purpose other than clinical work or training is prohibited.

Figure 7-5B. "Watch My Weight Go Down!" chart, filled in for a participant.

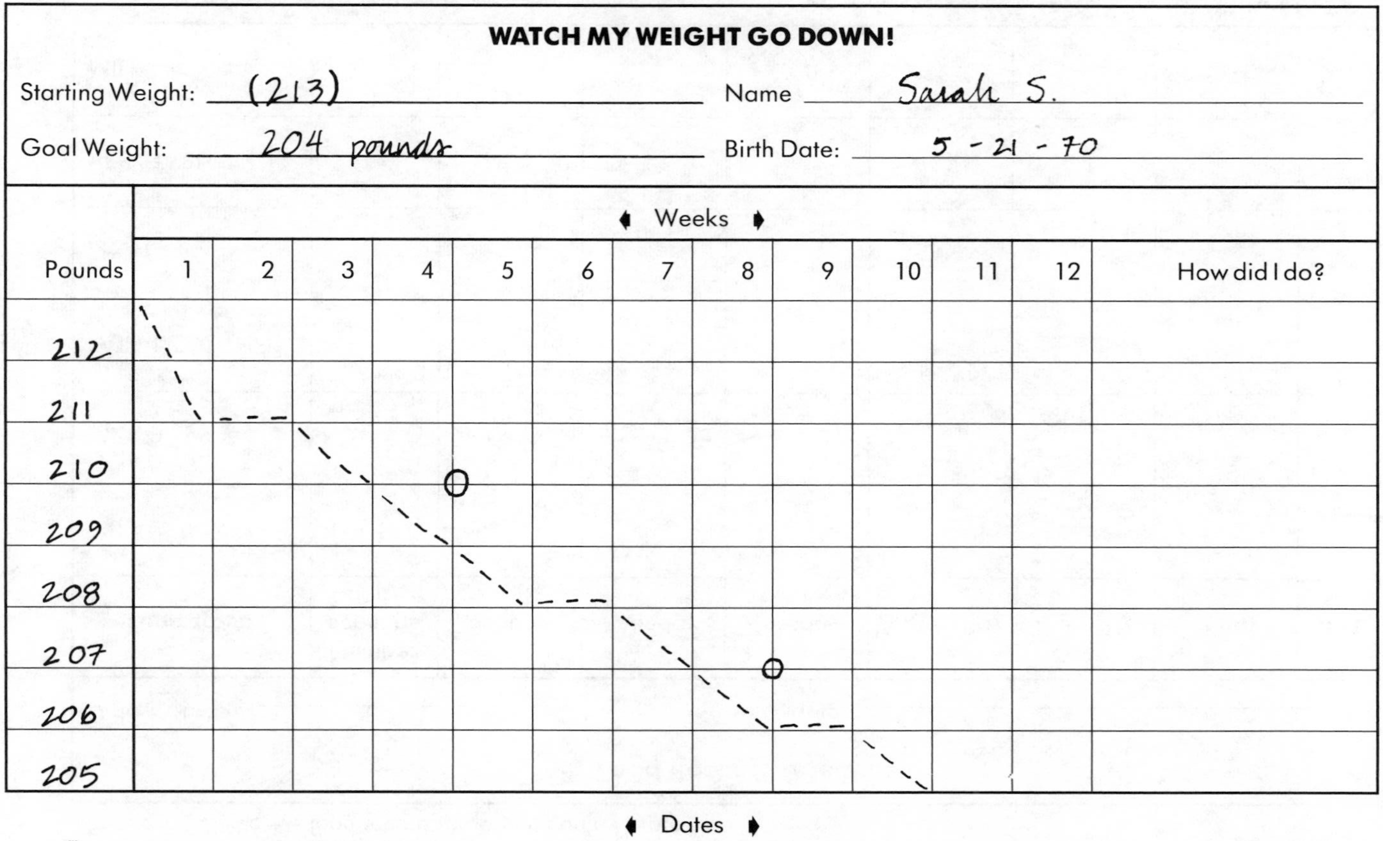

WATCH MY WEIGHT GO DOWN!

Starting Weight: ___(213)___

Goal Weight: ___204 pounds___

Name ___Sarah S.___

Birth Date: ___5 - 21 - 70___

Pounds	1	2	3	4	5	6	7	8	9	10	11	12	How did I do?
212													
211													
210													
209													
208													
207													
206													
205													

◆ Weeks ◆

◆ Dates ◆

Figure 7-6. Weekly food record for weight control program.

Food Record: One Week

Dates: From _____ to _____   Name _____

Food group	Number servings daily	Sunday	Monday	Tuesday	Wednesday	Thursday	Friday	Saturday
BREAD								
MEAT								
FAT AND OTHER								
FRUIT								
VEGETABLES								
MILK								

Figure 7-7. Example of a home assignment form for the weight control program.

HOME ASSIGNMENT

Return this date _____ Name _____

Exercise (stick figure)

Days of the week

1	2	3	4	5	6	7

Paste or mark a star on each day you exercised!

Activity

How did I do?

family choice after calculation of the caloric content of a base-line 3-day diet record. The latter is done when a computerized nutrition program is available. Some software designed for use in weight management programs is listed in Chapter 9.

Responsibilities of the Coordinator

The school staff person who coordinates the weight-control program needs to be a creative and enthusiastic leader, positive rather than punitive in attitude. The coordinator needs release time from other responsibilities to plan and conduct the program, including establishing recognition of significant accomplishments of the group with administrators, teachers, therapists, and students. Counselors, psychologists, and a nutrition consultant help the families to be supportive of their son, daughter, or roommate in making the changes in life-style that are essential to success in weight loss.

Achieving Weight-Loss Goals

The nutrition consultant and family should decide on the appropriate weight goal for each participant with consideration of the percentage of overweight, ability of the family and participant to change eating habits, types of food consumed, and activity level. The family member, along with the group member, needs to decide what is realistic. Short-term (monthly) goals should be set as well as the ten- or twelve-week weight goal. Present weight should be written in Figure 7–5, in first blank box. (Figure 7–5A is a blank form, and Figure 7–5B is filled in as an example.) The weight loss goal may be more or less than 1 pound each week. Weekly program goals are marked, as illustrated in Figure 7–6. The goal may be only a fraction of the person's total need for weight loss, but it should be a reasonable expectation, with success in its attainment more important than the total reduction in weight.

When the group members are young children, height as well as weight sould be considered. The growth graphs shown in Chapter 3 should be marked with a child's past years' measurements as a guide within the NCHS percentiles.

A beam balance scale is needed for accurate weights. Discussion following weighing-in is essential, so that group members can share their successes or problems, with the group offering praise or help to each member. Flexibility in presentation allows the program to be appropriate for groups of varying physical and mental capabilities.

Some learning units useful for the weight-control program are in *Curriculum for the Classroom*, Ch. 9. Figure 7–8 gives an example of an evaluation of a weight-control program.

Outcome of the Weight-Control Program

An award ceremony should be planned for the last session, with those who achieved their goals being especially honored, but all participants acknowledged for effort and attendance. Families, and in some facilities, the entire school share in the glow of success. Pictures of the group taken at this time can be a reflection of that success when compared to those taken at the first session.

Parents learn that they can expect their son or daughter to make good decisions about choices as to what they eat, their grooming, posture, table manners, and involvement in activities. Some parents are also pleased with their own weight loss!

Follow-up monthly meetings or another 12-week program usu-

Figure 7-8. Evaluation of weight control program form.

EVALUATION OF WEIGHT CONTROL PROGRAM

Group Name _____ Location _____

Starting date _____ Completed by _____

Facility meeting room:
1. Adequate furnishings including work tables, blackboard, balance scale, and space for exercises.
2. Attractive posters and other decorative items.

Program leader and other facility staff:
1. Attitude: enthusiastic, supportive, patient.
2. Preparation for and conducting program sessions.

Participants:
1. Attendance
2. Outcome in achieving weight goals:
3. Active participation in program:

Parents:
1. Attendance
2. Interest and cooperation demonstrated.

Nutrition Consultant:
1. Informative, innovative, consistent advice.

Summary:

Recommendations:

From *Nutrition and Feeding of the Handicapped Child*, by Iris M. Crump. © 1987 by College-Hill Press, a division of Little, Brown, and Company, Inc. Reproduction of this material for any purpose other than clinical work or training is prohibited.

ally is scheduled. Prevention programs have been developed for children who are at risk for overweight, such as those with Prader Willi or Down syndrome.

REFERENCES

Borjeson, M (1980). The etiology of obesity in children. In P.J. Collipp (Ed.), *Childhood obesity.* Littleton, MA: P & G Publishing.

Brinker, J.A. (1981). Behavior and metabolic factors in childhood obesity. In M. Lewis and L.A. Rosenblum (Eds.), *The uncommon child.* New York: Plenum.

Brownell, K.D., and Stunkard, A.J. (1980). Behavioral treatment for obese children and adolescents. In A.J. Stunkard (Ed.), *Obesity.* Philadelphia: W.B. Saunders.

Hartz, A., Giefer, E., and Rimm, A.A. (1977). Relative importance of the effect of family environment and heredity on obesity. *Annals of Human Genetics 41,* 185-193.

Khoury, P. (1983). Parent offspring and sibling body mass index association during and after sharing a common household environment. *Metabolism 32*(1), 82-89.

Rozin, P. (1980). Acquisition of food preferences and attitudes toward food, *International Journal of Obesity 4,* 356-363.

Society of Actuaries and Association of Life Insurance Medical Directors of America (1980). Build and blood pressure study, 1979, Volumes 1 and 2, Chicago, Society of Acturies.

BIBLIOGRAPHY: BOOKS ON WEIGHT CONTROL

Bower, Willard (1977). *Growing and thinking slim.* 2739 So. Whitney Blvd., Rocklin, CA 95677.

Brownell, K. (1979). *Behavior therapy for weight control: A treatment manual,* Dept of Psychiatry, University of Pennsylvania. 34th at Spruce, Philadelphia, PA 19174.

Ferguson, James M. (1976). *Habits, not diets: The real way to weight control.* Bell Publishing Co., Box 208, Palo Alto, CA 94302.

Jones, Jeanne (1972). *The Calculating Cook.* 101 Productions, San Francisco, CA.

Mayer, Jean. *A Diet for Living* (1977). Pocket Books (Division of Simon & Schuster), 630 Fifth Avenue, New York, NY 10020.

Satter, E.M. (1986). *Child of Mine: Feeding with Love and Good Sense.* Bull Pub. Co. Box 208, Palo Alto, CA.

Stuart, R.B. and Davis, B. (1977). *Slim Chance in a Fat World. Behavioral control of Obesity.* Research Press, 2612 North Mattis Ave., Champaign, IL 61820.

APPENDIX 7–1. Regimen for Weight Management

General Description

There will be 10 to 12 weekly group sessions for students in educable or learning disabled classes who wish to lose weight. The sessions will include activities and discussions that will help to attain goals and objectives. Participants will take responsibility for adhering to the program. Parents or caretakers will agree to help participants by providing appropriate foods and consistent encouragement to follow the program planned for them. School or program staff will plan and conduct the weekly group sessions with consultation from a nutrition consultant and school specialists, including a psychologist, nurse, recreation or occupational therapist, and administrator. Evaluation of outcome will also include specialists.

Criteria for Inclusion

1. Approval of physician or health care provider.
2. Children, adolescents, and adult persons in special education programs or other group settings for handicapped persons.
3. Participant's agreement to "contract" for weight loss according to program plans and individual goals.
4. Agreement of family of participant to support program plans.

Goals

The program goals are to:

1. Achieve ongoing weight management by gaining knowledge of food values.
2. Modify eating behaviors to attain positive habits.
3. Develop leadership and good judgment in decision making.
4. Improve self-image and social competence.
5. Attain greater agility through weight loss and exercise.

Objectives

1. Provide information that will help to make the diet regimen appealing and acceptable.
2. Practice positive eating behaviors in order to replace undesirable habits and establish long-term weight regulation.

105

3. Establish supportive counseling to avert or solve problems that could deter progress.
4. Plan group activities that help participants learn to enjoy the foods they need.
5. Maintain adherence to scheduled program through group dynamics.
6. Reward progress to reinforce adherence and promote enthusiasm.

Group Process

The weight control group will consist of persons who agree to attend 10 to 12 weekly group sessions. All participants will have physician's or health care provider's approval. Not less than 2 participants of the same sex will be in each group. Parents or caretakers will attend the first meeting and two additional meetings. The nutrition consultant will help to plan and implement the program, which will be conducted by facility personnel. Evaluation of program effectiveness will be made at mid-term and terminal sessions by nutrition consultant and facility personnel.

Nutrition Consultant Will Provide

1. Workshops to present the concept, outline the curriculum, and train the persons who will conduct the programs.
2. Initial diet planning and weight loss goals with group participants, parents, and program staff.
3. Consultation with the course coordinator and other contributors at regular intervals regarding the progress of each program.

The Facility Will

1. Plan space and time for the program.
2. Provide weight management program personnel to plan and conduct 10 to 12 weekly meetings for participants.
3. Select participants.
4. Contact families of participants (member of family is required to attend 3 meetings).
5. Monitor weights weekly.
6. Conduct meetings with parents.
7. Incorporate exercise program in the participants' school schedule.
8. Record program progress and evaluation of outcome.

APPENDIX 7–2. Outline Curriculum for Group Sessions of the Weight Control Program

Session I

Participants, Parents or Caretakers and
Nutritionist Introduction to Program

1. Why we want to lost weight. Group discussion.
2. How we lose weight.
   Nutritionist: describe "yes" and "no" foods.
   Review diet regimen using Select-A-Meal* booklet
3. Photograph and weigh each participant

Assignment. Learn to use Select-A-Meal diet plan.

Session II

Participants

1. Weigh-in and record weight on individual graphs.
   Weight graphs must be brought every week.
2. Set one-month and total program weight goals.
3. Personal meal planning
4. Introduce exercises.

Assignment. Bring pictures of "yes" and "no" foods. Do exercises daily.

Session III

Participants

1. Record weight on graph.
2. Fasten pictures of "yes" and "no" foods to poster board and discuss these foods.
3. Play game, matching food models to foods shown in the Select-A-Meal booklet.

---

*American Diabetes Association, North Carolina Affiliate, Inc. Station Square, Ste. 50, Rocky Mount, NC 27801

* All Sessions Conducted by School Personnel

4. Practice exercises to music with group members taking turns leading the group.

<u>Assignment.</u> Practice exercises daily. Identify foods served at mealtime throughout the week with Select-A-Meal personal meal plan.

Session IV

Participants

1. Record weight on graph.
2. Participants point out foods they had last week as shown in Select-A-Meal.
3. Participants discuss and select a name for their group and make name tags.
4. Practice exercises.

<u>Assignment.</u> Practice exercises daily. Help plan a day's menu at home.

Session V

Participants

1. Record weight on graph.
2. Select menus from the food models and discuss selection.
3. Practice exercises.

<u>Assignment.</u> Practice exercises daily to music. Participants are to initiate their own exercise period during half-hour TV or radio program or while playing a favorite record.

Session VI

Participants

1. Record weight on graph.
2. Share ways in which they have reached their goals.
3. Demonstrate and practice good grooming.

<u>Assignment.</u> Exercise daily. Practice grooming tips demonstrated. Take card to parents or caretakers, notify-

ing them of next week's meeting that they will attend. Cards should also be mailed home the day following this session by group leader.

Session VII

Participants, Parents or Caretakers
and Nutritionist

1. Record weight on graph.
2. Demonstrate exercises.
3. Nutritionist reviews progress.
4. Discuss making plans for a party at the end of the group sessions. This party is for the entire group and will honor those who have achieved their weight goals. The type and location of party will be decided by the group; for instance, picnic, bowling, or miniature golf.

Assignment.   Practice exercises daily. Bring party ideas to next meeting.

Session VIII

Participants

1. Record weight on graph.
2. Discuss dental health and how it relates to diet.
3. Practice exercises.
4. Discuss choices for party.

Assignment.   Exercise daily. Practice tooth brushing techniques.

Session IX

Participants

1. Record weight on graph.
2. Observe and practice nail care.
3. Practice posture, how to walk, how to sit down gracefully in front of a mirror.
4. Vote on type of party to be held.

Assignment.   Exercise daily. Practice nail care and posture.

Session X

Participants

1. Record weight on graph.
2. Plan the party; participants form committees. Suggestions for committees are: planning, purchasing, preparation, and decoration.
3. Practice exercises.

Assignment.   Exercise daily. Work on party assignment.

Session XI

Participants

1. Record weight on graph.
2. Assess knowledge of food choices by letting the participants set up typical meals with the food models. Other group members comment on the meals shown.
3. Practice exercises.

Assignment.   Exercise daily. Each day practice grooming and posture. Take card to parents or caretaker notifying them of next week's meeting which they will attend. Group leader should also mail cards home the following day reminding parents of the meeting.

Session XII

Participants, Parents or Caretakers, and Nutritionist

1. Record weight on graph.
2. Photograph each participant.
3. Joint meeting with parents to discuss exercise, grooming, and weight charts and reaching weight goals. Encourage successful group members to tell who helped them and how. What pleases them most about their weight loss? (New clothes? Appearance? Ability to run faster, to be chosen for a ball team? Praise?)
4. Complete party plans.

CHAPTER 8

The Successful School Mealtime

Iris M. Crump

PREPARATION FOR THE MEAL

Specific techniques and foods for individual problems are described elsewhere in the book. The objective of this chapter is to observe the mealtime atmosphere. Schools often have no elaborate dining areas and the eating process may be dreadfully messy, but, hopefully, a pleasant situation can be created so that meals are enjoyable. A few reminders are appropriate and are pictured and listed.

1. Arrange a pleasant environment:
   - limit noise
   - keep groups small
   - minimize traffic and other distractions
   - use colorful dishes and food
2. Make the child comfortable:
   - in an appropriate chair
   - with feet on the floor or footplate
   - with trunk and head supported, if needed
   - head tilted slightly forward

111

- with tray or table placed at elbow and waist level if child sits well
- use dry clothes, bib, or napkin, as appropriate
3. Present foods attractively:
   - Serve at appropriate temperature.
   - Separate items. Do not mix foods together even if mashed.
   - Serve small amounts, with more available if desired.
4. Provide appropriate equipment:
   - spoon to fit child's mouth, plastic coated if bite reflex is present
   - divided plate if food is mashed or pureed
   - cup with lid or spout
5. Feed, or guide self-feeding with awareness:
   - Face the child at eye level.
   - Name the food items and encourage acceptance by the child.
   - Allow adequate time for optimal intake.
   - Praise the child for doing well.
6. Give yourself a pat on the back!

ADAPTATION OF THE SCHOOL FOOD SERVICE

There is frequently a lag in age-appropriate eating skills of the handicapped child. Delayed development, tactile defensiveness, motor problems, and aberrant behaviors need to be identified and treated. Frequently, mealtime is used as a therapy session: the danger is that the child will associate stress and anxiety with food as outcome of therapy, and resist meals. *Caution is necessary to avoid misuse of the mealtime for therapy. All skills that the child has developed should be used consistently, but the singular function of meals is for nourishment.* Greatly improved success results from using existing skills at mealtime and scheduling oral therapy at another time. Weight loss and poor health can be the outcome if the child cannot eat the food presented. The child may actually be hungry when the meal is over. Table 8–1 suggests appropriate management of mealtimes for the child with delayed eating ability.

SPECIALIZED STAFF AND EQUIPMENT

Mealtime should be a pleasant experience, with social interaction between students, and between student and feeder for the child who cannot feed himself. Time allowance for meals must be

Table 8–1. Menu Planning with Adaptations for Handicaps

Group Level	Developmental Skills	Description of Food and Equipment	Sample Menu Breakfast	Lunch
I	Poor suck; tongue thrust or retraction Poor lip closure Weak head, trunk control	Pureed or blended food Liquids slightly thickened Five to six feedings daily Vitamin supplement	Orange juice, thickened with Sustagen® or Meritene®. Cream of wheat Milk Yogurt	Puree of turkey, rice, with margarine Puree of squash with margarine Puree of peaches Milk with Sustagen®
II	Good suck; bottle and spoon fed Lateral tongue movements; no chewing Sits upright with support Drinks from cup with lid and spout without consecutive swallowing	Junior or ground soft meat. Mashed cooked vegetables Mashed fruit Cooked whole grains *Soft* scrambled egg Three meals with nourishment	Orange juice Cream of wheat Scrambled egg Milk	Puree of turkey on rice with margarine Banana squash, mashed with margarine Puree of peaches Milk
III	Up-and-down chewing motion Developing lip closure Drinks from small mouth cup or glass, consecutive swallow, no spilling Takes food from spoon with upper lip Visual location of dish Hand-to-mouth coordination	Chopped food of soft texture Soft raw fruit, bite size Graham crackers, Arrowroot or vanilla wafers Liquids with and between meals 3 meals, liquid nourishments	Orange juice Cream of wheat Scrambled egg Milk	Chopped turkey in gravy on rice Banana squash, diced, with margarine Graham crackers Peaches, mashed Milk

(continued)

113

Table 8–1. (continued)

Group Level	Developmental Skills	Description of Food and Equipment	Sample Menu	
			Breakfast	Lunch
IV	Rotary chewing Bites off pieces of soft food Drinks without spilling Holds cup or spoon, hand on hand Finger feeds with raking motion Good eye contact. Names some foods.	Bite-size foods (no skin, raw greens or nuts) Some finger foods every meal Stabilized dish Cup with 2 large handles 3 meals, evening nourishment	Orange juice Scrambled egg Toast with margarine Milk	Bite size turkey in gravy on rice Banana squash Bread, margarine Peaches, bite size Milk
V	Competent bite, chew, Swallow Can drink with straw Self-feeds with spoon Holds cup but does not return it to table unaided Asks for food or drink	Full diet Generous clear liquids between meals Utensils appropriate, dish stabilized Tray or table at elbow height 3 meals with evening nourishment if needed	Orange juice Scrambled egg Toast, margarine Milk	Turkey, bite size, in gravy on rice Banana squash Cole slaw Bran muffin Peaches, bite size Milk
VI	May stuff mouth Handles cup well Finds his place at table. Serves self appropriately Uses fork well Appropriate behavior Names foods, states preferences	Full diet, tasty and colorful Generous clear liquids between meals 3 meals, evening snack if appropriate	Orange juice Scrambled egg Toast, margarine Milk	Turkey in gravy on rice Banana squash Cole slaw Bran muffin Peach slices Milk

extended for the handicapped child. Special equipment or adapted utensils help the child to become more self-reliant. The occupational therapist helps with selecting appropriate tableware, and the physical therapist adapts chairs and tables for successful mealtimes. The speech therapist will have worked with the student during therapy sessions to improve oral function, and demonstrated the techniques to teaching staff. Teachers, aides, and volunters nurture close daily rapport with the students; mealtime is a significant period because of the immediate food reward.

Menu Adaptations for the Soft Diet

When a food on the regular menu cannot be adapted to the soft diet, a substitution of similar nutritive value must be provided. The food service department should not be expected to always prepare a separate menu, but to have modifications that meet school lunch requirements. A list of suggestions is shown in Table 8–2.

Cautions and Quick Tips

Weiners are the most common cause of choking in young children. They should be cut into thin strips or circles. Peanut butter is a valuable food, but should not be put in a sandwich for children who chew poorly. The bread and spread become gummy and can cause choking. Peanut butter is delicious in oatmeal, or mixed with mayonnaise (to dollop on chopped banana or applesauce), or in pudding or cookies (don't grimace - try it!).

Jello is difficult for a child with poor tongue control to chew — it slips down his throat and he gags. Just fork-mash it and mix with mashed fruit or cookie crumbs.

Many casserole entrees can be blenderized or pureed. Macaroni and cheese, however, becomes a sticky paste that is inedible and must be replaced with another entree.

Fruits and vegetables that are cooked instead of served raw have lost all of their vitamin C and part of certain B-complex vitamins. These nutrients need to be replaced to meet the school lunch requirements and the child's needs.

Nutrient content of foods that are strained, pureed, or blenderized have been reduced by the addition of liquid necessary for the processing. A larger portion must be served to provide the nutrients required. Fiber from fruits and vegetables is lost in strained foods, but not in blenderized or mashed items.

Jello, yogurt, ice cream, and blenderized fruits can be consi-

Table 8–2. Suggested Soft Food Substitutions of Similar Nutritional Value

Main Menu Offering	Alternate
Beef burrito or taco	If ground beef is used, brown it, then add cream soup and simmer. Shredded beef should be ground, then creamed. Serve on rice or noodles.
Chef salad	Cottage cheese, tomato soup
Chicken or tuna salad	Creamed chicken or tuna, with rice
Hamburgers	Meatballs (crumbs or oatmeal and egg in ground beef, simmered at least 20 minutes) with mashed potatoes
Hot dogs	Omelet or soft-scrambled egg with sweet potatoes
Sandwiches	Junior chicken or beef baked with (instant) mashed potatoes, egg added.
Raw apples	Baked or cooked apples
Raw celery & carrot sticks	Cooked carrots, mashed or chopped
Raw cherries	Canned, cup-up cherries
Cole slaw	Cooked finely-shredded cabbage
Corn on the cob	Cream-style canned corn
Raw whole grapes, raisins, prunes	Ground or finely cut, cooked fruit
Melon wedges	Watermelon cubes, mashed melon
Whole oranges, grapefruit	Segments without membrane
Pineapple	Mashed papaya or banana
Salad green	Mashed avocado or cooked spinach

dered liquids of high-nutrient density. Remember that children enjoy good tastes as much as you do; make the food palatable, attractive, and mealtime pleasant.

DEALING WITH DIFFICULT CHILDREN

Oral therapy is often a frightening experience for a child who has been on tube feeding, had oral surgery, or is neurologically damaged and tactilly defensive. There may be no apparent oral defect so that normal function is expected. Rejection of the food or willful resistance may be suspected, when the problem may be fear or extreme tactile discomfort, both of which reinforce each other.

Case Study

Two-year-old Alex is a severely battered child who is now in a foster home. He is the height of an 18-month-old and is extremely thin. He avidly seeks affection, but mealtime was once terrifying: he had been force-fed, resulting in discomfort and regurgitation. When he appeared to be trying to vomit, his nose was flicked by the foster mother, causing him to gasp, and thus arresting the regurgitation. He was overfed — the former foster mother continued forcing strained food "until his stomach is tight," in her words. He was not gaining weight because of early deprivation, both prenatally and during infancy. Therefore, his digestive tract is deficient in enzymes and absorptive surface. When placed on a nutritional supplement and in a child-development program, he gradually learned to feed himself and trust the staff. He now enjoys soft foods and never regurgitates, but will not allow others to feed him.

Specialized equipment should be explored for the physically impaired student. There are a number of important reasons for requesting an evaluation by an occupational or physical therapist to assess the child's potential for self-feeding and recommend equipment that would facilitate learning:

1. The child will gain self confidence by learning self feeding. There is no greater glow on the face of a child than when he gets food to his mouth unaided, albeit half of the spoonful ends up on face, bib, and floor!

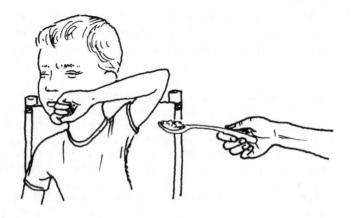

2. He is more likely to eat foods he previously rejected when being fed, because now he is in control, rather than being threatened by someone else's decision as to what goes into his mouth.
3. As the child develops skill in self feeding, more time will be available for the teacher or aide to help other children.
4. Parents can let their child self-feed for a longer period of time each meal than if they are doing the feeding, allowing more food to be consumed by the underweight child.
5. The child will not feel as "different" as when fed, and can have his meal with other children rather than being fed after they have finished eating.

Adaptation of regular utensils and dishes is preferable. The child and parents will feel he or she is less handicapped if the same dishes are used as the rest of the class. The plate may be fastened to the table with an "octopus" soap holder. The spoon handle may be slipped into a thick foam-rubber cover, or the spoon's bowl may be twisted to facilitate scooping.

MANAGEMENT OF INAPPROPRIATE BEHAVIOR AT MEALTIMES

The goal of a successful mealtime is a comfortable, cooperative child who enjoys the meal, and a feeder who is pleased with the relationship of nourishing the young charge, no matter how messy the task. The suggestions made in this section summarize the care plans of psychologists, child-development specialists, teachers, parents, and nutritionists.

Dilemma: Refusal to be Fed

Adam is physically disabled, and therefore, is limited in decisions he can make in self-help skills. Someone may push him in his wheelchair to where they want him to be; others dress him; still others feed him. Adam may be able to get finger food or an adapted spoon to his mouth, but teacher feels that he does not get enough food when self-feeding exclusively. He strongly resists her feeding him.

HOW-TO. In Table 8–1, developmental skill IV includes foods to finger-feed, along with others that are spoon-fed. Adam can have a bowl of finger foods in front of him. The teacher will *hold* the dish of spoon-foods with the understanding that he will have help in eating it. Hand-on-hand spoon feeding follows. Both Adam and teacher are successful; he has his food to eat independently and does not expect to finger-feed from the dish the teacher holds. It may take several days, but if a favorite food is in the teacher's dish, and the teacher is adamant about "helping," Adam usually consents.

Dilemma: Regression of Self-Feeding

Ben has no speech. Understanding why he behaves in an inappropriate manner is even more difficult than anticipating the nonhandicapped child's responses at mealtime, because he cannot explain what he is thinking or feeling. The feeder may not know Ben's skills or preferences. Attitudes and skills recognized in the therapy and home settings should be discussed with the feeder so that Ben's optimal function is expected. Ben prefers to be fed because severe spasticity makes self-feeding a difficult task. He may pretend illness or inability. Also, he may want to get the exclusive attention of the feeder.

HOW-TO. The feeder can ask Ben to show how he eats, point out which dish and cup he likes, and indicate *how much* (not *what*) he wants of each food. (The "one-bite-of-each" holds even in this setting.) Ben may like the challenge and has succeeded this first time in getting additional attention, but the feeder has not allowed him to manipulate the situation. Ben will usually want to show off his ability if the feeder praises him for all he *can* do, but not reprimand him for his reluctance to feed himself.

Dilemma: Resistance to Chewing

Progress in accepting increase in texture of food may be slow, taxing the patience of teaching staff when they see no oral defect. The speech therapist or occupational therapist can explain procedures to both teachers and parents so that they can be consistent in their feeding of the child. Parents or caretakrs then become part of the training team. It should be remembered that they must be comfortable with the plan, particularly if physician and friends are criticizing the child's poor weight-gain.

Susan's parents feel that she will eat less, that she will become resistive, and their valuable role of nourishing and sharing a pleasant mealtime will be destroyed. Yet, without their cooperation, Sue will not succeed in learning and accepting the new procedure. *No parents will change their feeding pattern if they fear that their child will be less well-nourished using the new plan.*

HOW-TO. The nutritionist can prescribe an appropriate supplement with the physician's approval. The team can be assured that their recalcitrant student, Sue, will not suffer, even if she eats less of the textured food. They do not create a tense mealtime while Sue is gradually learning to enjoy a greater variety of table foods. The formula can be a home-prepared supplement, which can be a usual part of Sue's meal, but not replace other food. If Sue wants formula only instead of food at mealtime, it can, rather, be given on arrival at school, arrival home, and at bedtime.

Dilemma: Dawdling with food

Jon is an 8-year-old boy who has a repaired myelomeningocele and a shunt for hydrocephalus. He is in an orthopedically handicapped class that is served lunch in the regular school cafeteria. Jon tends to be overweight, although he plays with his food at lunch, eating only small amounts.

HOW-TO. Jon's food preferences and eating habits at home should be discussed with his parents. Jon's activity level is low due to his preference to move around in his wheelchair instead of on crutches. Therefore, his energy (caloric) expenditure is low. Jon's mother expects him to eat the same amount as her other two sons. Jon's appetite is poor; he is very picky. His mother lets him have whatever he wants at mealtime, concerned that "he doesn't eat enough food," in her words. She also grieves because he cannot run and ride a bicycle like her other sons. Therefore, she lets him spend his time eating any snacks he requests.

The school nurse can discuss the damaging long-term effects of indulgence and overweight on both health and self-image. Alternative activities, such as games, guests, crafts and books, instead of food after school and evenings should be planned. Jon's mother should not buy the snack foods Jon wants. If only fruits and vegetables were available for snacks, Jon could not be begging for candy, sodas, and chips.

When Jon's parents follow-through with these plans and enlist Jon's brothers' help, Jon will be hungrier at school lunchtime. It is likely that he will eat better. Jon may also be getting extra attention for not eating. His tray should be emptied at the same time as the other students whether or not he has eaten. No special urging or replacing of items should be allowed.

A vitamin–mineral supplement should be given daily until Jon is eating a good variety of foods as recommended in Chapter 1.

The school may have a weight-management program as described in Chapter 7. If he joined the group, Jon would get added attention, self-esteem, and improved mobility because of weight loss. Jon's parents would join other parents in feeling good about changing food habits and helping Jon in a valuable way.

Dilemma: Persistent Behavior Problems

Persistent aberrant behaviors at mealtime should be observed and discussed by the school team including the psychologist and nutrition consultant. An examination by a physician familiar with developmentally disabled children may be appropriate. There may be a medical problem limiting appetite, taste sensation or digestion. (Defects of the esophagus are not readily detected.)

Robert is a 6-year-old boy who is an example of oversight of a physiological problem. The foster mother accomplished more than was ever expected, getting him off nasogastric tube-feeding onto oral feeding, although the doctors advised a gastrostomy. Robert has scant tongue mobility and poor lip closure. He had taken pureed food only until he started attending a special education class of children at trainable level of development. His learning ability was shown by his competent use of a complex communication board. His mouth looked intact, but Robert strongly resisted eating solid foods. It was thought that the foster mother permitted him to continue on pureed food because he was very under-weight for his height and her primary concern was to have him gain weight. When he was force-fed soft foods, he regurgitated the food and became very fearful of attending school. Extensive examination disclosed an extremely narrow esophagus made almost impassable by enlarged tonsils. Tonsillectomy and dilitation of the esophagus have been done, but Robert is now terrified of spoon feeding and subsists mainly on a special formula. Extensive retraining will be necessary to reassure Robert that he will not be hurt again.

CHAPTER 9

Nutritional Education Programs in the Classroom

Iris M. Crump
James O. Cleveland

Seventy years ago, good health was designated as the number one objective under the seven cardinal principles of education by the United States Office of Education. That declaration has been upheld by many studies including the 1968 White House Conference on Food, Nutrition and Health. In 1969, the final report stated, "The intake of appropriate and adequate foods and their effective utilization by the human body is the cornerstone of human growth and development to provide the basis for the maximum fulfillment of each individual's potential."

The Massachusetts public schools conducted a survey the year that report was published. Approximately 80,000 students in elementary schools recorded a 24-hour food intake. Data was compared to a food pattern developed by the United States Department of Agriculture called the *Basic Four*. This pattern of food groups was designed to provide a well-balanced diet, as defined in the RDA of the Food and Nutrition Board of the National Research Council, National Academy of Science. The data showed that only 45 percent of the children ate the daily recommended 4 servings

123

of fruits and vegetables. About 72 percent consumed the milk allowance, and 63 percent met the requirement for intake of high-protein foods. A large percentage, 72, ate 3 or more servings of concentrated sweets that contributed negligible nutrients because they consisted mainly of "empty calories." The significant deficits in meeting recommended food intakes prompted measures that included increased nutrition education in the school curriculum. The outcome of the data caused increased funding and concern for the important role nutrition plays in the learning process.

Many curricula for nutritional education have been published. (See references at the end of this chapter, and Chapter 10.) The California State Department of Education established an extensive Nutrition Education and Training Program (NET) in 1980. The goal was to enable school staffs and students to learn to make wise food choices that would contribute to life-long well being. One of the NET curricula selected for publication and dissemination addresses students in special education. This curricula is entitled *Growing Up Healthy**.

The need for nutritional education of students has been shown to be urgent. The child with a handicap faces problems that further complicate the process of remaining well-nourished. School staff can encourage development of positive attitudes in students who are handicapped (including children who are severely mentally retarded) toward eating wholesome foods. Acceptance of nourishing meals can be significantly improved by including some appealing presentations about good food in classroom curriculum. The following section will address nutrition education of handicapped students.

INDIVIDUAL EDUCATION PROGRAMS

It is the intent of the Federal Legislature and Public Special Education agencies that individuals with exceptional needs are provided their rights to appropriate programs and services which are designed to meet their unique educational needs as required by Public Law 94-142.

Individual Education Programs (IEPs) are required for all children receiving special education services in the public schools. The provisions of the IEP, as specified by the Act (PL 94–142) and the regulations, are two-fold: (1) the actual IEP meeting, when school

---

*Obtained from Nutrition Project, Redwood Coast Regional Center, 808 "E" Street, Eureka, California 95501.

personnel and parents jointly make decisions about the child's program; and (2) the IEP document, which is the written record of the decisions made at the IEP meeting.

Some of the purposes and functions of the IEP include the following:

1. It is a vehicle for facilitating communication between the parents and school personnel regarding the child's needs, what will be provided in relation to those needs (and by whom), and what the anticipated outcomes may be.
2. It provides an opportunity for the IEP team members to become better acquainted with the student's needs and program and resolve any concerns or differences of opinion that might exist.
3. It is an opportune time to clarify any procedural protections that are available to parents.
4. It is a specified time to establish in writing a commitment of resources needed to complete the special education and related services identified on the IEP.
5. It should create a compliance, monitoring, and management system for parents, school personnel, and others responsible for insuring that the child's educational needs are being met.
6. It becomes an evaluation device to measure the progress made by the child.

In preparation for an IEP Conference, the child's parents should make a list of concerns and other issues they want to discuss at the forthcoming meeting. The IEP meetings are sometimes time limited, and such a list will assure that all desired issues are attended to at that meeting. If a "list" is made over a period of time prior to that meeting, parents are more likely to include information helpful to the IEP team, than if it is hurriedly prepared before the meeting. This type of participation and on-going involvement by the parents enhances the level of communication desired by the school staff, and allows for better carry-over of the child's program objectives.

The child should be involved in the IEP meeting whenever possible. The better they understand their nutritional and dietary problems, the more able they will be to assist in the "plan of action" and accept some of the responsibility for ongoing planning and maintenance.

The content of the individualized education program for each child, as specified in Part B, Education of the Handicapped Act, as amended by PL 94–142 (121a.346) include:

1. A statement of the child's present levels of educational performance.
2. A statement of annual goals, including short-term instructional objectives related to those specified goals.
3. A statement of the specific special education, instruction, and related services required for the child.
4. The extent to which the child will be able to participate in regular educational programs.
5. The projected dates for initiation of services and the anticipated duration of the services.
6. Appropriate objective criteria and evaluation procedures and schedules for determining, on at least an annual basis, whether the short-term instructional objectives are being achieved.

The following includes some examples of how recommendations related to various nutritional and dietary issues can be expressed in child's IEP. Examples are based on problems covered in the previous chapters.

Case Example: Ted

Ted is a 7-year-old boy who has severe spastic cerebral palsy (described in Chapter 3). He is 43 inches tall and weighs 32 pounds. His parents and teacher are keenly aware of the difficulties he has in feeding. It is a real challenge to feed a "resistive" child, which usually takes at least a half-hour to complete, a task that can be tedious and messy for both parties involved. Ted's weight gain and general health are critically poor, so proper nutritional intake must be considered when designing his IEP. The IEP team will include the parents, teacher, school nurse, occupational therapist, nutritionist, and social worker. The date of the IEP will be October 10, 1986.

Goal

Improve weight gain and general health (See Figure 9-1).

Example: Susan

Susan is a 3-year-old girl who suffered a head trauma resulting in left hemiparesis. She is nonambulatory and wheelchair bound. Susan is an only child of Spanish-speaking parents. Her weight

Figure 9–1. Individual education program for Ted, a 7-year-old boy with severe spastic cerebral palsy.

INDIVIDUAL EDUCATION PROGRAM

Objective 1.0
Evaluate Ted's present and potential level of feeding skills by 11/15/86.

Plan 1.0
Teacher will refer to feeding clinic by 10/15/86 (feeding clinic includes occupational therapist, physical therapist, and speech pathologist).

Plan 1.1
Teacher to coordinate meeting of staff involved and members of the feeding clinic, following assessment to plan feeding training.

Objective 2.0
Special feeding equipment needs to be identified and procured by 1/15/87.

Plan 2.0
Physical therapist will refer Ted to California Children Services for adaptation of wheelchair by 12/18/86.

Plan 2.1
Occupational therapist to adapt and provide feeding utensils for Ted by 1/10/87.

Objective 3.0
Increase Ted's weight by 3 pounds by 1/15/87.

Plan 3.0
School nurse to refer Ted to nutritionist for dietary assessment by 10/15/86.

Plan 3.1
Teachers and parents to record all Ted's food intake for 3 consecutive days (2 school days and 1 consecutive weekend day) by 11/2/86.

Plan 3.2
Nutritionist to assess nutritional status and nutrient intake by 11/15/86. Make recommendations.

Plan 3.3
School food service management and teacher to modify school meals, as recommended, by 11/15/86 (Parents to be advised re: home meals.)

Plan 3.4
School nurse to weight Ted once each month and report weight to teacher and parents, 11/15/86, 12/15/86, 1/15/87.

Objective 4.0
Ted's health status to be recorded and reported to Ted's physician by 1/15/87.

Plan 4.0
Parents and school nurse to record Ted's illnesses, weight change, and send written report to Ted's physician on 11/15/86; 12/15/86; 1/15/87.

gain has been too rapid: at 43½ inches (88 cm) in height, she is below the 5th percentile for height. She weighs 34 pounds (15 kg), which is above the 50th percentile for weight. Her mother reports that Susan will continue to eat as long as someone will feed her, and cries when they stop feeding her. Susan is on anticonvulsant medications. The IEP meeting is scheduled for October 10, 1986. Those attending the meeting will include the teacher, school nurse, occupational therapist, nutritionist, resource specialist. The parents are invited, but have always failed to appear, giving transportation problems as the reason.

Goal

To change Susan's weight so it will better coincide with her height (See Figure 9–2).

Example: Terry

Terry is a 19-year-old student who is mildly mentally retarded and lives with her parents. She is enrolled in a work-study program. Terry has a severe seizure disorder that is controlled by medications. She is 63 inches (160 cm) tall, at the 25th percentile for height and weighs 210 pounds (95 kg), far above the 95th percentile for weight. Her appropriate weight for her height is 112 pounds (51 kg). She has gained 40 pounds in the last 3½ years. Terry tends to be sedentary and avoids contact with other people due to her overweight condition. She is anxious to lose weight so she will feel more free to go swimming and dancing. Nutritional assessments have been done. The IEP conference will be held on November 10, 1986. Those attending will include Terry, the teacher, parents, nutritionist, educational consultant, social worker, recreation therapist, and the school nurse.

Goal

To control Terry's weight gain so that her weight coincides with height (See Figure 9–3).

Many times it is beneficial to the child who has the nutritional and dietary problem, and that child's classmates, for the problem to be discussed by the teacher and the students. Other students can be very supportive and it resolves "differences" from becoming an additional problem or concern.

Classroom posters and displays can be used to encourage good eating habits, appropriate foods for special diets, and the promotion of general good health.

Figure 9–2. Individual education program for Susan, a 3-year-old girl with left hemiparesis.

INDIVIDUAL EDUCATION PROGRAM

Objective 1.0
Maintain Susan's weight at 34 pounds until her height is close to 37 inches.

Plan 1.0
Teacher will refer Susan to nutritionist for assessment of caloric and nutritional intake by 10/15/86.

Plan 1.1
Teacher will schedule a conference for nutritionist to meet with parents (and interpreter) when the assessment report is ready. Recommendations for food intake at home will be written in Spanish for parents. (Recommendations for meals at school will be sent to school food service management).

Plan 1.2
School nurse will weigh Susan monthly and send report to teacher, nutritionist, and parents

Objective 2.0
Susan's physician will be apprised of her dietary assessment, results, and recommendations by 11/1/86.

Plan 2.0
Nutritionist will contact Susan's physician and discuss recommendations regarding her weight-program.

Objective 3.0
Susan will be fed more slowly to achieve satiety with less food consumption by 11/10/87.

Plan 3.0
Teacher will invite parents to observe eating lunch at school by 11/15/86.

Plan 3.1
Teacher will team-feed Susan while feeding 2 other students in order to extend feeding period by 11/15/86.

Plan 3.2
Susan will immediately be taken to another area in the room when feeding is completed in order to signal "end of meal."

Figure 9–3. Individual education program for Terry, a 19-year-old who is mildly mentally retarded.

INDIVIDUAL EDUCATION PROGRAM

Objective 1.0
Terry will lose 1–2 pounds per week during the next quarter period of the school year (end of February 1987).

Plan 1.0
Nutritionist will consult with Terry's physician regarding an appropriate reducing plan by 11/15/86.

Plan 1.1
Terry will follow a 1200 calorie daily diet plan at home and school.

Plan 1.2
School's staff will support Terry's diet plan by suggesting alternative foods that are more appropriate than the choices she has been making.

Objective 2.0
Terry will join a weight-management group at school 1/4/87.

Plan 2.0
Recreation therapist will organize and conduct a weight management group (with consultation from the nutritionist) to meet weekly, by 1/4/87.*

Plan 2.1
Terry's parents will participate in the weight management group with Terry.

---

*See Chapter 7, Appendix 7–1, Regimen for Weight Management.

CURRICULUM FOR THE CLASSROOM

The strategies needed in designing instructional goals and sequences for the handicapped child are more complex than those used for children without handicaps. The teacher cannot assume that all sensory and motor capabilities are intact, or that the level of mental or physical integrity has been accurately established. Also, few classes have homogeneity of physical or mental capabilities, so planning equivalent or analogous activities for the lesson objective is limited to the ability of the least competent student or must offer several levels of practice-learning activities.

Some examples of instructional goals and sequences for nutritional education are offered here, including prerequisite competencies. They are purposely varied in format so that they can be adapted to a variety of curriculum designs. They are suggestive rather than exhaustive examples that address some of the IEP objectives given in the first section of this chapter, and some nutritional education needs expressed in Chapters 6 and 7.

Curriculum Approach #1

CONTENT AREA GOAL: The student will develop a sense of excitement and adventure in learning about food.

GOAL STATEMENT: The student will name and taste a nutritious food that is unfamiliar.

COMPETENCY: Visual and auditory abilities: 15-minute attention span; hand and arm mobility. Kindergarten level.

LEARNING EXPERIENCE: *Please don't eat the daisies,* a story-hour presentation of new foods. Example: broccoli.

"Do we eat flowers like these?" (Show pictures of daisies or roses,) "No! Never!"

"We *do* eat *one* kind of flower!" (Show broccoli plant or stalk) "Its name is broccoli. Can you say 'broccoli'?"

"We eat *only* this flower that mother buys or grows for us. Broccoli grows like other flowers. Let's pretend we can make some grow."

Show shadow picture, slides, pictures, or a demonstration.

Shallow box, hole in center
Cardboard sheet over hole
Sand in box
Cardboard box, open side,
   hole in top

Pantomine or demonstrate planting seeds. "First, we plant seeds. We cover them with soil."

"What makes the plant grow?" (Children hand-pantomine watering the "ground," sunshine, and rain.)

"It takes time to grow while you are busy." Children hand-pantomine sleeping, eating, playing, and singing. This activity is repeated as plant appears and again it "grows." (The cardboard sheet removed, and the broccoli thrust gradually upward through a hole.)

"It is ready to pick and eat!" Have ready some washed "flowers" of broccoli to offer children to taste or take home to show the family.

FEED-BACK. "The following day say, "Do you remember the name of this flower?" Offer *one bite* of cooked broccoli with lunch. Talk about how it tastes. Do not criticize comments indicating dislike or strangeness. Encourage the attitude of "new, and different."

ASSESSMENT: The next week, include broccoli in the lunch menu. Note verbal and taste responses.

Curriculum Approach #2

CONTENT AREA GOAL: Students will develop an understanding that daily food intake is related to maintaining good health.

GOAL STATEMENT: Students will name (or otherwise indicate) conditions of good health. Students will name some foods that contribute to good health. Kindergarten and first-grade level.

COMPETENCIES: Visual and auditory competence; 20-minute attention span; verbal or pointing identification of healthful food.

LEARNING EXPERIENCE: Students will look at pictures of healthy children, including some in wheelchairs. Teacher will name signs of good health: lustrous hair, clear skin, pink color of lips and nail beds, firm teeth and gums, appropriate weight for height, and smiles.

FEED-BACK: Students will point to and state (if possible) signs of good health in other pictures. They will point to themselves, also, as wanting to be healthy.

A box labeled *YES Foods* containing plastic or paper models of healthful food is passed so that each child can draw out and identify a food. For the nonverbal student, the teacher can say, "Is it an apple? or carrot?" so the child can nod or smile the correct answer. Other students may want to help a child who cannot pick-up a model.

A second box labeled *NO foods* containing items high in sugar and fat is offered by the teacher with discussion of dental damage, excess weight, and missing healthful foods as results of their frequent use. Children may say, "But I like that." The teacher can suggest that they pick an alternative food from the YES box. Children should not be taught that foods in the NO box should never be eaten, but rather that they should be eaten only occasionally after YES foods have been selected.

FEED-BACK: Fishing game: A paper clip is fastened to the back of fish-shaped construction-paper pieces having a food picture on the opposite side. A dowel with string and magnet is the fishing pole. Each child "catches" a fish, turns it over, identifies the food picture and places it in the Yes or No box. The other students decide if it was the correct choice.

Curriculum Approach #3

CONTENT AREA GOAL: Students will develop eating patterns that contribute to wellness.

GOAL STATEMENT: Students will explain and use the seven food groups in the weight-control program.

COMPETENCIES: Visual, auditory, and cognitive skills to understand food groups and a personal meal plan. Competencies at 4th grade level.

LEARNING EXPERIENCE: Students will each have a Select-A-Meal®* booklet to work with throughout a 10-to-12 week program for weight control. Program outline and conduct is in Chapter 7. The first session is with the nutritionist, who explains the booklet to participants and their parents or roommates after discussion of the program plan. The assignment for both students and parents is to take the Select-A-Meal to the table at mealtime to identify the food groups the meal provides.

The second session is largely occupied with the personal meal plan and setting of program weight goals. Exercises are introduced. The assignment for home study for students is to demonstrate which foods they should and should not eat by accumulating Yes and No food pictures to bring to the 3rd session.

The 3rd session concentrates on what group members have learned about their diet. Plastic food models are available from Nas-

---

*American Diabetes Association, North Carolina Affiliate, Inc., Station Square, Ste. 50, Rocky Mount, NC 27801

co®*, in portion sizes described in Select-A-Meal®†. Paper food models by Dairy Council®‡ are somewhat similar in portion sizes. These models and the participants' individual folders (described in Chapter 7) should be available for the 3rd session. Cafeteria trays, each labeled with a picture of one of the food groups should also be ready.

Students examine their folders and tell about the food pictures they have brought, which are then deposited in their folders.

The food models always fascinate the students: as they examine them, they can put them on labeled trays to demonstrate their knowledge of the food groups. Group members prompt each other by this session, and leadership is emerging. This quality is used throughout the remaining sessions. The reticent students, however, should also be given responsibilities appropriate for their abilities.

FEEDBACK: The following group of sessions of the weight control program reinforce learning acquired by session 3, and demonstrate the competence of the students in using the food groups in Select-A-Meal.®†

Curriculum Approach #4

CONTENT AREA GOAL: Students will use equipment needed in developing skills for independent living.

GOAL STATEMENT: Students will learn how to count and measure ingredients using kitchen tools.

COMPETENCIES: The visual, auditory, and cognitive skills to follow picture directions (literacy at 2nd-grade level). The ability to hold cups and spoons.

LEARNING ACTIVITIES: Equipment needed:

1. Tables, chairs, blackboard, chalk, work sheet, and pencil
2. A set of 4 measuring cups and 4 snap-apart measuring spoons for each student
3. Dry beans and animal crackers
4. Sandwich bags, paper towels, and 1" diameter gummed circles

---

*Nasco, Fort Atkinson, WNI, 53538

†American Diabetes Association, North Carolina Affiliate, Inc., Station Square, Ste 50, Rocky Mount, NC 27801

‡National Dairy Council, 6300 NO. River Rd. Rosemont, IL 60018-4233

Students are asked to line up their cups in order of size, i.e., largest, next largest, smaller, smallest. Repeat the descriptive words as they work.

Show students the size markings on the cups, i.e., 1 cup, ½ cup, ⅓ cup, ¼ cup. Draw exaggerated pictures of cups of 4 graduated sizes on the blackboard and write the size inside each, as on the students' cups. Give students each four gummed circles and a pencil. Ask them to write the four sizes on the circles and glue them onto the handle of the appropriate cups. (The task is visual memory; they will not understand the size relationships at this time.)

Give students numbered worksheet (pages 136 –137) to complete, to confirm their counting skills. Ask them to write their names on the sheets. Collect these when completed.

Ask students to count out five animal cookies. When completed, they may eat them.

Students will clean work area.

A useful follow-up would be a copy of the activities for the students to take home for further practice of measuring foods.

Evaluation and transferrence of learning are use of measuring skills in preparation of a food from a recipe that uses similar measurements. It is important that the students in the weight control program learn to take resonsibility for planning and preparing some foods in their diet that they can share.

Many picture recipe books feature dessert and other high-calorie foods unsuitable for persons who need to limit calories. All of the following curriculum background materials are appropriate for the weight control program.

When lunches are sent from home, it is difficult to keep calories under 300, which should be the maximum at noon. The following picture recipes offer foods that meet the personal meal plan lunch pattern, but are suitable for all other students as well.

calorie foods unsuitable for persons who need to limit calories. All of the following curriculum background materials are appropriate for the weight control program.

When lunches are sent from home, it is difficult to keep calories under 300, which should be the maximum at noon. The following picture recipes offer foods that meet the personal meal plan lunch pattern, but are suitable for all other students as well.

Curriculum Approach #5

CONTENT AREA GOAL: Students will develop skills that prepare them for independent living.

Draw a line

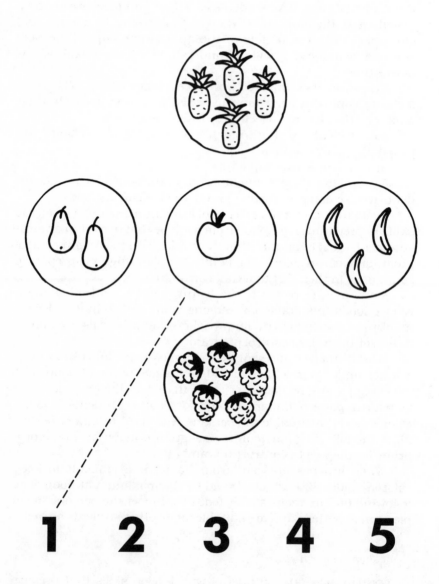

1 2 3 4 5

Count them . . .

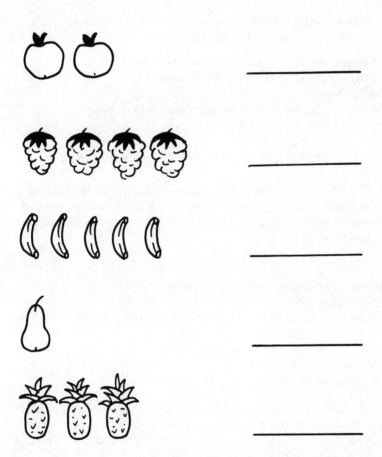

Fill in the blanks.

GOAL STATEMENT: Students will follow a recipe in preparation of a wholesome food.

COMPETENCIES: The visual, auditory, and cognitive skills to follow picture directions (literacy at 2nd grade level). The ability to hold cups, spoons.

LEARNING ACTIVITIES: Equipment needed: Food preparation classroom, aprons, recipe, and foods indicated on recipe (pages 139 – 143).

- Student will prepare recipe as instructed.
- Student will store or eat food as instruted.
- Student will clean utensils and work area.
- Recipe can be sent home with students to repeat.

PUBLICATIONS FOR THE SCHOOL FACULTY

There are excellent publications that address nutritional education and training of students, school staff and parents. A few resources appropriate for those with special needs are described in this section.

Client Assessment and Intervention
Materials Distribution
Rehabilitiation Research and Training Center in
Mental Retardation
2nd Floor Clinical Services Building
University of Oregon
Eugene, OR 97403

A series of manuals are offered for mildly and moderately retarded adolescents and adults to learn practical skills for living in the community. A guide for the curriculum is *Independent Living Skills Teacher's Manual.* The manuals are:

- Budgeting and Bill Paying
- Nutrition and Menu Planning
- Grocery Shopping
- Personal Hygiene
- Household Management and Home Safety
- Simply Cooking
- Cooking (to accompany Simply Cooking)

(text continued on page 144)

Ham and Cheese Sandwich

Equipment:
Knife

Ingredients:
2 slices bread
1 tblsp. reduced calorie
    salad dressing
lettuce
1 slice of ham
1 slice of cheddar cheese

1. Spread salad dressing on
   1 slice of bread.

2. Trim fat off ham and
   place on bread.

3. Slice cheese and place on ham.

4. Place washed lettuce on
   cheese. Cover with other
   slice of bread.

5. Cut sandwich in half.

Low-Calorie Molded Salad

Equipment:
1 quart pan
measuring cups
serving spoon
timer

Ingredients:
1 diet soda (lemon-lime)
6 packets Equal®
1 package Knox® gelatin
        (unflavored)
1 can crushed pineapple

1. 1 package Knox® gelatin

½ cup cold water

2. Pour ½ cup of cold water
   into pan.
   Put gelatin into water.
   Stir all the time over low
   heat for 3 minutes.
   Turn heat off.

3. Add 1 can diet soda
   (lemon-lime)

Add 6 pkts Equal®

Stir.

Equal® - G.D. Searle and Co
Knox® - Knox Gelatine Inc.

4. Put it into refrigerator for 20 minutes.

5. Drain crushed pineapple. Measure 1 cup.

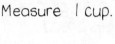

6. Pour gelatine mixture and pineapple into bowl. Stir.

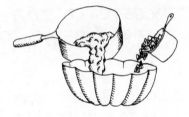

7. Put it into refrigerator until firm.

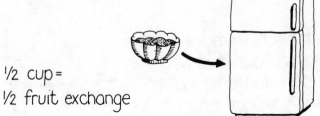

* ½ cup = ½ fruit exchange

Skinny Egg Salad Sandwich

Equipment:
I quart pan
cutting board

Ingredients:
2 eggs
¼ tsp. lemon juice
⅓ cup cottage cheese
(low fat)
¼ cup dill pickles
2 slices bread
(whole grain)

1. Carefully place 2 eggs in saucepan. Add water to cover eggs.

2. Place pan on stove burner. Turn heat to high.

3. Bring water to boil (water in pan will bubble). Then turn heat to medium and cook eggs for 10 minutes.

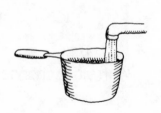

10 min.

4. **Turn off heat.** Remove pan from stove. Pour hot water out of pan. Run cold water into pan to cool eggs. Peel eggs.

5. Chop eggs on a cutting board.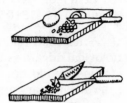

6. Chop ¼ cup dill pickle.

7. Put chopped food into small mixing bowl.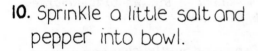

8. Add ⅓ cup cottage cheese.

9. Add ¼ tsp. lemon juice.

10. Sprinkle a little salt and pepper into bowl.

11. Stir well.

12. Spread ½ of egg mixture on a slice of bread. Cover with another slice of bread. Mixture makes enough for 2 sandwiches.

    I sandwich = 2 bread exchanges
                   1 meat exchange

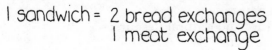

Feeding the Handicapped Child
Child Development Center
University of Tennessee
711 Jefferson Avenue
Memphis, TN 38105

This book relates to the scientific, educational, and technological advances influencing the food habits and nutritional status of children. The nutritional needs of children with an interdisciplinary approach to specific problems are discussed.

Growing Up Healthy (NET Program)
North Coast Regional Center
808 E Street
Eureka, CA 95501
Attn: Nutrition Education Project

The main goal of *Growing Up Healthy* is to provide special education students with the nutrition knowledge and skills needed to be healthy and live as independently as possible, by using curriculum materials in a team approach that involves teachers, parents, and food service staff. The content areas covered include food choices, food handling (cooking skills), and consumer competencies (shopping skills).

Guides for Nutritional Assessment of the Mentally Retarded and the Developmentally Disabled
Child Development Center
University of Tennessee Center for Health Sciences
Memphis, TN 38163

This guidebook contains recommendations that promote high-quality nutritional services and a draft of assessment forms for evaluation of both the nutritional status and level of eating development of persons who are developmentally disabled.

Nutrition for Young Children: A Correspondence Course
Cooperative Extension Service
U.S. Dept. of Agriculture
College of Agriculture and Natural Resources
University of Connecticut
Storrs, CT 06268

A series of 6 lessons are designed to help teachers, other school staff, and parents learn about growth and development, nutritional needs, and eating skills of young children.

Nutrition Simulation
EMC Publishing
300 York Avenue
St. Paul, MN 55101

This computer activity using the Apple series provides practice for orthopedically handicapped students in the skills of meal planning with economics in mind. The 3 parts include a "spending spree," menu planning, and food choices with cost, calories, and nutritional quality in mind.

Resources for Nutrition and Food Services Education
Nutrition and Food Service Education Resource Center
3221 Wallace Avenue
Vallejo, CA 94590

An annotated list of materials available from the resource center that has a collection of articles on microfiche, as well as pamphlets and programs pertaining to nutrition. Among the topics included are nutritional education from infant through secondary school; nutrients, requirements, and deficiencies; snacking, and children's food habits; dental health, parent education and community involvement.

School Nutrition and Food Service Techniques for Children with Exceptional Needs
Publication Sales
California State Department of Education
P.O. Box 271
Sacramento, Ca 95802

Guidelines for food service personnel, teachers, aides, volunteers, and parents and concerning eating difficulties of students with handicaps. Techniques are offered that many solve some problems.

What I Usually Eat
National Dairy Council
Rosemont, IL 60018

This computer program is designed for students with 3rd to 6th grade competencies. A one-day food intake is analyzed by food groups. Individual or classroom printouts are available.

101 Picture Recipes and Teacher's Manual
Association for Retarded Citizens/Ottawa County
246 S. River
Holland, MI 49423

Resources for Nutritional Services

Kathryn Brune

Among the many resources available for nutritional services are those (1) controlled by federal, state, and local governments; (2) controlled by private agencies; and (3) trade associations with nutritional programs. In this chapter, descriptions of these various resources are included.

PROGRAMS CONTROLLED BY FEDERAL, STATE, AND LOCAL GOVERNMENTS

There are many state, local, and national resources that have a direct effect on the health of every individual and family residing within their jurisdiction. Since services vary for each agency, the general functions of each operation will be listed. Addresses for these agencies can be obtained from your local health department.

Department of Health and Human Services (DHHS)

Following are operations under the control of the DHHS:

OFFICE OF DISEASE PREVENTION AND HEALTH PROMOTION (ODPHP). The ODPHP is the center of the DHHS for policy development and coordination of activities related to the prevention of disease, maintenance of health, and the promotion of sound health practices.

OFFICE OF CONSUMER AFFAIRS. The Office of Consumer Affairs is charged with the responsibility of handling inquiries for the FDA, and also serves as a clearinghouse for their consumer publications.

PUBLIC AFFAIRS. The office responds to requests for information on the human service programs administered by the Office of Human Development Services.

NATIONAL INSTITUTE OF CHILD HEALTH AND HUMAN DEVELOPMENT. The Institute conducts and supports basic and clinical research in maternal and child health and the population sciences. It responds to individual inquiries on related topics, such as studies on developmental biology and nutrition, mental retardation, and developmental disabilities.

ADMINISTRATION FOR CHILDREN, YOUTH AND FAMILIES (ACYF). Inquiries are answered by using publications from various offices of the ACYF on the subjects of child abuse, day care, domestic violence, and the Headstart program.

BUREAU OF HEALTH CARE DELIVERY AND ASSISTANCE (BHCDA). The BHCDA serves as a national focus for efforts to ensure delivery of health care services to both residents of medically underserved areas and special groups.

DIVISION OF MATERNAL AND CHILD HEALTH. The Division administers grants to state health agencies for maternal and child health and Crippled Children's Services. Funding is also provided for special projects of regional and national significance.

PRESIDENT'S COMMITTEE ON MENTAL RETARDATION. The Committee advises the President on appropriate ways to provide for mentally retarded citizens and to prevent this type of disability. Areas of concern are prevention of biomedical and environmental causes of retardation, community support services, international activities, and public information.

HEADSTART. Provides nutritional, medical, dental, mental health education, and social services, mainly for pre-school children, starting from age 3. The objective of Headstart is to help children from low-income families achieve social competence by overcoming the handicap imposed by poverty.

WOMEN, INFANTS AND CHILDREN (WIC). WIC is a special supplemental food program. It provides nutritious food supplements to pregnant, breast feeding, and postpartum women, as well as to infants and children up to their 5th birthday. WIC is operated by authorized health facilities such as the American Red Cross, the Department of Public Health, Community Health Centers, and hospitals.

Department of Agriculture

Following are operations under control of the Department of Agriculture.

FOOD AND NUTRITION INFORMATION CENTER. This agency was established to serve the information needs of persons interested in human nutrition, food service management, and food technology. The Center acquires and lends books, journal articles, and audio-visual materials dealing with these areas of concern. The collection ranges from children's books to the most sophisticated professional materials.

HUMAN NUTRITION INFORMATION CENTER (HNIS). The HNIS conducts research in food and nutrition to improve professional and public understanding of the nutritive values of foods and the nutritional adequacy of diets and food supplies.

NATIONAL SCHOOL LUNCH AND BREAKFAST PROGRAMS. The programs help schools serve nourishing low-cost meals to children. In addition to cash assistance, participating schools get USDA-donated foods and technical guidance.

Library of Congress

The following agency is under the control of the Library of Congress.

NATIONAL LIBRARY SERVICE FOR THE BLIND AND PHYSICALLY HANDICAPPED (NLS). The NLS comprises a network of 56 regional and 103 local libraries working in cooperation with the Library of Congress to provide a free library service to persons who are unable to read or use standard printing materials because of visual or physical impairment. The NLS delivers books and magazines in recorded form, or in Braille, to eligible readers by postage-free mail. The NLS also provides information on blindness and physical handicaps upon request.

Information Specialists

There are two agencies under the control of Information Specialist.

NATIONAL INFORMATION CENTER FOR HANDICAPPED CHILDREN AND YOUTH (NICHCY). The NICHCY acts as a center to facilitate the flow of information and ideas about young people with handicaps among the people who are concerned about them. The NICHCY is designed to serve parents, disabled adults, and professionals who work with handicapped people. The NICHCY is especially interested in the needs of rural areas, culturally diverse populations, and severely handicapped people.

NATIONAL MATERNAL AND CHILD HEALTH CLEARINGHOUSE. The National Maternal and Child Health Clearinghouse is the centralized source of materials and information in the areas of human genetics, and maternal and child health.

Communication Division

The Communication Division controls the following agency.

PRESIDENT'S COMMITTEE ON EMPLOYMENT OF THE HANDICAPPED. The Committee strives to eliminate environmental and attitudinal barriers impeding the opportunities and progress of handicapped persons.

Department of Education

The Department of Education controls these agencies.

CLEARINGHOUSE ON THE HANDICAPPED. The Clearinghouse serves two purposes: to respond to inquiries from handicapped individuals, and to serve as a resource to organizations that supply information to and about handicapped persons.

REHABILITATION SERVICE ADMINISTRATION (RSA). The RSA was created to administer federally sponsored and supported vocational rehabilitation programs for physically and mentally disabled persons.

ERIC CLEARINGHOUSE ON TEACHER EDUCATION. The Clearinghouse acquires, evaluates, abstracts, and indexes journal and research literature in two subject areas: the preparation and development of education personnel, and selected aspects of health, physical, and recreational education.

PROGRAMS CONTROLLED BY PRIVATE AGENCIES

There are a number of nongovernmental organizations that have community nutrition programs or other nutrition components. They include voluntary health agencies, professional organizations, organizations connected with business and industry, and foundations. This section briefly describes the various *nutrition programs available* through these private agencies.

Quasi-Government Agencies

AMERICAN NATIONAL RED CROSS (ARC). ARC conducts relief operations in major disasters and in smaller local emergencies. In addition, local chapters may carry on various programs that are broadly designed for the promotion of health and prevention of disasters. Two activities are of particular significance to community nutritionists: preparation and service of food in quantity and under emergency conditions, and provision of public education and advisory assistance in food and nutrition.

AMERICAN DIABETES ASSOCIATION (ADA).
The present activities of the ADA are under four major programs: (1) public education and detection, to alert the public to the early signs of disease and find unrecognized cases; (2) patient education, to teach the patient about the disease and its control; (3) professional education, to provide information to physicians and other professional health workers on treatment; and (4) research, to find methods of prevention and cure.

AMERICAN HEART ASSOCIATION (AHA). The objective of the AHA is to support research, education, and community service programs to reduce death and disability from heart disease. AHA has a program of education for the public and various professionals; it finances research, carries on many kinds of community services, publishes pamphlets and professional journals, and provides films and speakers.

NATIONAL FOUNDATION-MARCH OF DIMES (MOD). The MOD sponsors research, health service, and education programs to prevent birth defects and otherwise improve the outcome of pregnancy. MOD considers malnutrition during the prenatal period as a major factor in low birthweight and mental retardation, and emphasizes the importance of diet.

Private Agencies

UNITED CEREBRAL PALSY ASSOCIATION (UCP). The function of the United Cerebral Palsy Association is to people with cerebral palsy and their families with needed services that are not provided by existing programs. The services that UCP provides include: information and referral, public information and education prevention, parent education and counseling, and regular parent seminars.

EPILEPSY SOCIETY. The services provided by the Epilepsy Society include:

- Information and referral to sources of medical, social, vocational, legal, and financial aid
- Group and individual counseling for people with epilepsy and their families
- Prevocational and vocational counseling
- Employment consultation for adults with epilepsy
- Consultation services to professionals, agencies, schools, and employers having contact with persons with epilepsy
- In-service training for professionals who work with the person with epilepsy
- Child classroom educational programs

NATIONAL SOCIETY FOR AUTISTIC CHILDREN. The Society supports medical and psychological research, provides emergency family services, consultation, evaluation and referral, and protection and advocacy. The Society also aids in respite care and habilitation information, social and recreational activities, community and professional education, and dissemination of literature.

ASSOCIATION FOR RETARDED CITIZENS (ARC). The goal of the Association is to provide services that enable retarded persons to live happy, satisfying, and useful lives. Direct services of the Association include: work activity programs, vocational trade training programs, infant development programs, sitter service, outreach to Black and Mexican-American communities, client advocacy, Special Olympics, and camping programs.

Hospitals and Community Clinics

Local hospitals and community clinics provide many services to individuals, some of which include group programs for weight management, heart disease, diabetes, substance abuse, hypertension, and basic nutritional needs.

TRADE ASSOCIATIONS WITH NUTRITIONAL PROGRAMS*

The Trade associations have several groups that are involved in nutritional programs.

AMERICAN INSTITUTE OF BAKING (AIB). The AIB is an educational and research organization. It conducts basic education in nutrition and prepares materials suitable for use in community nutrition programs.

CEREAL INSTITUTE. The Institute conducts both research and education in nutrition and the role of cereals in the diet. It can supply film strips, leaflets, pamphlets, posters, and other teaching materials to schools, health organizations, and similar agencies, as well as nutritional data on cereal products.

EVAPORATED MILK ASSOCIATION. The Association prepares printed materials and film strips for nutritionists, teachers, and others, covering the uses and labeling of evaporated milk, as well as infant feeding.

---

*Data compiled from Obert, J.C. (1978). *Community Nutrition*, John Wiley and Sons, New York, pp. 121-123.

NATIONAL CANNERS ASSOCIATION. The Association prepares educational materials for home economists, food editors, and teachers, and gives information on the nutritional value of canned foods and their use in the diet.

NATIONAL DAIRY COUNCIL (NDC). The NDC has state and local groups with staff nutritionists who conduct community nutritional programs in their areas. The programs developed cover educational events for nutritionists, dietitians, teachers, and other professionals. The NDC also conducts research and educational programs on eating habits using the four-food group approach.

NATIONAL LIVESTOCK AND MEAT BOARD. The Board promotes, educates, and provides information about meats. It conducts recipe testing, supplies materials to the media, and publishes teaching materials for classroom use.

Glossary

antigenic: immunogenic; having the properties of materials that induce resistance and/or sensitivity to toxic substances.

apoenzyme: the protein portion of an enzyme.

athetosis (dyskinesia): a condition in which there is a succession of involuntary writhing or jerky movements, which may be more evident during voluntary activity.

bolus: chewed piece of food which has been turned into a mass, ready for swallowing.

bone age: assessment of age of the skeleton, done by interpreting a roentgenogram of the hand and wrist.

catabolic: relating to the breakdown in the body of complex compounds into simple ones. The opposite chemical reaction is the anabolic reaction, or building up of body substances.

centimeter: 0.3937 inch: one one-hundredth of a meter.

central nervous system (CNS) disorder: any of a variety of motor, sensory, and/or cognitive disorders, caused by an insult or injury to the immature brain or nervous system.

cerebral palsy (CP): "Sometimes called chronic, nonprogressive neurologic injury, is a disorder of muscle control or coordination resulting from injury to the brain during its early (fetal, perinatal, and early childhood) stages of development. There may be associated problems with intellectual, visual, or other functions. The problem lies in the brain's inability to control the muscles; the muscles themselves and the nerves connecting them to the spinal cord are perfectly normal. The extent and location of brain injury determines the type and distribution of CP."*

cholesterol: the steroid that is most abundant in animal tissues. It can be synthesized in humans as well as absorbed from food.

coenzyme: a substance that catalyzes enzymes or is essential to enzymatic activity. Vitamin coenzymes include thiamin, riboflavin, nicotinic acid, pantothenic acid, pyridoxine, cobalamin, pteroylglutamic (folic) acid, and biotin.

congenital anomalies: mental or physical traits, deformities, or diseases existing at birth.

dyskinesia (athetosis): a condition in which there is a succession of involuntary writhing or jerky movements, which may be more evident during voluntary activity.

electrolytes: compounds that can be dissociated into ions. Sodium (Na), potassium (K) and chloride (Cl) are the major electrolytes in the human body.

Food exchange list: classification of foods based on similarity of nutrient composition. Any food in the group can be interchanged with any other food in the group.

hemiparesis: paralysis or other dysfunction affecting only one side of the body.

holoenzyme: the complete enzyme, comprised of coenzyme and apoenzyme.

homeostasis: a state of balance in the body; equilibrium of chemical composition and function of body fluids and tissues.

homogeneous: of uniform structure throughout.

hyperperistalsis: overactive wave-like involuntary movements that push food through the digestive tract.

hypoxia: lack of adequate oxygen for adequate respiratory functioning.

kilocalorie: the amount of heat required to raise the temperature of 1 kilogram of water 1 degree centigrade. This is the *large Calorie* used in nutrition. The *small calorie* is used in physics.

linear growth velocity: the rate of growth in length of a segment or whole body.

metabolic disorder: disturbance of physical and chemical changes within living cells.

metabolite: a product of metabolism, normal or abnormal.

nutrient density: an index of food quality based on the U.S. Recommended Daily Allowance (RDA) for each nutrient, described

---

*From Blackman, J. (1983), *Medical aspects of developmental disabilities in children birth to three.* Iowa City: University of Iowa Press.

as an allowance per 100 kcalories.

nutritional status: state of the body resulting from intake and assimilation of nutrients, determined by clinical, biochemical, dietary, and anthropometric evaluations.

osmolality: the osmotic concentration of a solution, determined by the ionic concentration of dissolved substance per unit of solvent.

osteomalacia: softening of the bones.

strabismus: inability of one or both eyes to focus on the same object, due to muscle incoordination.

synthesis: the process of forming complex compounds from simpler substances, such as proteins from amino acids.

tactile defensiveness: aversion to touch, related to an over- or undersensitivity of the tactile system.

transplacental: through or across the placenta, from which the fetus receives its nourishment.

triceps skinfold measurement: measurement by calipers of the subcutaneous tissue over the triceps muscle of the arm; closely correlated with body weight.

wheal: a round elevation of the skin, as from an insect bite or intradermal injection.

INDEX